NEW AMERICAN FURNITURE:

The Second Generation of Studio Furnituremakers

NEW AMERICAN FURNITURE:

- - - - - -

The Second Generation of Studio Furnituremakers

MUSEUM OF FINE ARTS, BOSTON · **EDWARD S. COOKE, JR.**

Library of Congress Catalogue Card Number 89-63204
ISBN: 0-87846-315-1

Typeset by Monotype Composition Company
Printed by Franklin Graphics
Designed by Janet O'Donoghue

The exhibition and catalogue have been made possible by grants from the
National Endowment for the Arts, a federal agency.

Exhibition dates

Museum of Fine Arts, Boston
December 8, 1989–March 11, 1990

Renwick Gallery of the National Museum of American Art,
Smithsonian Institution
April 20–September 3, 1990

PHOTOGRAPHY

All color photography was done by the Museum of Fine Arts, Boston, Department of Photographic Services. Black and white photographs were supplied by lenders.

Photo credits

Museum of Fine Arts, Boston, Department of Photographic Services: pp. 32, 36, 40, 44, 48, 50 (fig. c), 52, 56, 59, 60, 64, 68, 72, 76, 80, 84, 88, 92, 96, 100, 103, 104, 108, 112, 116, 120, 124, 128

David Arky: pp. 130, 131
J. Ahrend: p. 42
David Caras: p. 82 (fig. c)
Chris Cunningham: p. 46
George Ermel: p. 39
Brian Gulick: p. 70
Bobby Han: p. 115
Greg Heins: p. 83
Thomas Kneebone: p. 114 (fig. b)
Alphonse Mattia: p. 78 (fig. b)
Tom Millea: p. 91
Garry Okazaki: p. 75
Morse/Peterson: p. 47
Dean Powell: pp. 66, 67, 78 (fig. c), 79, 102
Nicoli Zurek: p. 38

PREFACE

"New American Furniture" demonstrates the Museum's commitment to contemporary three-dimensional arts. Although our Department of American Decorative Arts and Sculpture strives to show the full range of American furniture history, and though we have assembled the largest and most distinguished collection of contemporary studio furniture of any major museum, we have never before invited a group of artists to conceive and create furniture for a temporary exhibition.

This show grew out of the enthusiasm of Jonathan L. Fairbanks, the Katharine Lane Weems Curator of American Decorative Arts and Sculpture, and Edward S. Cooke, Jr., assistant curator of American decorative arts. Recognizing a revival of interest among studio furnituremakers in historic design and furniture, they invited twenty-six leading furnituremakers to Boston for a two-day symposium in October 1987. The symposium highlighted ethnic traditions, production techniques, varying concepts of function and social use, and the status of the craftsman, as well as historic design sources. The sessions were characterized by a lively exchange of ideas among furnituremakers from across the nation, who represented a broad variety of stylistic approaches. Each furnituremaker was encouraged to take inspiration from a particular piece in the collection—whether from a decorative detail, nomenclature, or social use—and to make a new work specifically for inclusion in this exhibition.

It took considerable courage to plan an exhibition for which none of the works yet existed, but the artists rose to the challenge. Many produced their best work to date. This dazzling array of extraordinarily well-crafted objects celebrates the plurality and diversity of American artistic production today, and demonstrates the Museum's ongoing involvement with art at the cutting edge.

Alan Shestack
Director

FOREWORD

Like all mass movements that surrender the individual to autonomous archetypes, the mass production of furniture has had benefits for society at large, but its dark side has been the eclipse of much personal creative energy. Against the impersonal qualities of manufactured society, the studio or small shop movement has survived and remains a potent moral force and provides new directions.

Not many generations ago it was customary for artists and artisans to advertise that their works were in the latest fashion or style. For most of the twentieth century, however, adherence to ephemeral fashion has been considered a pursuit unworthy of serious artists, many of whom believe that their works transcend style or fashion. Fashion changes slowly or quickly according to shared values of a culture, but concepts of beauty inevitably change. Subtle shifts in these cultural values allow curators and historians to date objects. Yet the notion of freedom from reference to historical styles and the belief in the discovery of eternal principles of design was one of the central tenets of modern art theory. The new attitude might be described as abstract design without historical references—an ahistorical approach towards design.

The beginnings of this new attitude can be traced to the crafts-design reform movement beginning with the Crystal Palace exhibition in London in 1852. Forward-looking critics at that time deplored the overly ornate products displayed at that exhibition. Although the ornamentation of primarily functional objects was popular at the time, critics felt that the use of excess ornament inspired by antique sources was dishonest. Pioneers of Modernism advocated the stripping away of ornament that made reference to past styles. Critic and botanist Christopher Dresser recommended that designers and craftsmen study the structure of plants and flowers in order to discover and apply universal principles of geometry and proportion to the design of everyday objects.[1] While Dressser did not discount the value of studying masterpieces from the past, he encouraged artists and designers to search for fundamental principles rather than merely imitate the surfaces of objects made in past times. The design principles discussed by Dresser, Owen Jones, and others profoundly influenced the decorative arts of the late nineteenth and early twentieth centuries—periods called by later art historians the Aesthetic Movement and the Arts and Crafts Movement.[2]

In *A Theory of Pure Design*, published in 1907, Dr. Denman Ross advocated an approach to design that was totally free of historical references.[3] A painter, lecturer at Harvard, trustee of the Museum of Fine Arts, Boston, and major contributor to the Museum's collections, the author was well known for the amazing range of his taste and his collections. Although trained as a professional historian, Ross approached design non-historically, illustrating principles of harmony, balance, rhythm, symmetry and other abstractions in his book with spots, lines, and other graphic devices. He was convinced that the same principles applied to painting, architecture, sculpture, and the decorative arts. For Ross, art was the expression of beauty, and its mission was to seek order and beauty for the sake of order and beauty. This form of art for art's sake was, to Ross, the artist's religion.

Other writers of the period also advocated non-historical approaches to design. For example, Ernest A. Batchelder, a ceramist from Pasadena, California, explained in his *Design in Theory and Practice* (1910) that, while European countries had enjoyed distinctive national traditions, Americans had "no traditions; in which fact is our best hope."[4] He believed that American designers and artists were unfettered by the past, and could therefore boldly strike out for "an elementary basis on which to build." For Batchelder, beauty—indefineable though universal—had "no style or period or country"; it was an ahistorical ideal, constant and everlasting, free from tides of taste or fashion.

Following the First World War, new production techniques combined with the new ideal aesthetic theory to challenge the small shop that handled custom furniture. Two basic trends—one more traditional and one more futuristic—appeared at the 1925 Paris Exposition Internationale des Arts Décoratifs et Industriels Modernes.[5] The former featured the superb workmanship of elegant and richly figured wooden furniture made by hand in custom shops that tended to draw upon traditions of the past. By contrast, the incorporation of such man-made products as steel, chrome, glass, and other industrial materials was considered the progressive side of furnituremaking by the 1930s. This direction was particularly well-suited for the development of large-scale factory production. The question of materials rather than style began to engage many critics, among them Edwin Avery Park. In *New Backgrounds for a New Age*, Park noted that, although wood had been used in the past, many Americans were attracted to new directions and materials: "We crave to be based on here and now, only we can't find footing in the confusion."[6]

The confusion noted by Park stemmed from the continued popularity of antique styles for some of the domestic market and the acceptance of new industrial designs for office and domestic markets. The immigration of progressive designers to America in the 1920s and early 1930s, especially after the Bauhaus closed in 1933, stimulated interest in modern fashion. At the two world fairs (Chicago, 1933 and New York, 1939) Americans were offered almost every kind of manufactured product shaped with sleek edges, streamlined contours, and fresh, bright hues. At the same time, however, Colonial Williamsburg was undergoing restoration and such collectors as Henry Francis duPont and Francis Garvan were building major collections of colonial American furniture. Eighteenth-century and early nineteenth-century styles remained popular sources for furniture design.

The tenacity of the colonial style and its emphasis upon the aesthetic qualities of wood grain and craftsmanship caught the attention of the furniture designer T.H. Robsjohn-Gibbings. In *Good-bye, Mr. Chippendale* he predicted that furniture for the future would be made of wood with grain left natural but enhanced with lacquer. This wood furniture was to be plain, comfortable, and designed to fit the body. Robsjohn Gibbings claimed that such an emphasis on function had "never really [been] attempted before."[7] While historically inaccurate, this statement reflects a new faith in the possibilities of furniture that was shared by the makers of the new wooden furniture in the studio movement that emerged in the late 1940s and early 1950s. In reaction to the great quantity of factory-made furniture in modern and colonial styles, the studio furnituremakers Wharton Esherick, George Nakashima, Sam Maloof, Walker Weed, Arthur Carpenter, and Tage Frid all found personal ways in which to express their affection for wood and to make comfortable and beautiful furniture following abstract or ahistorical design principles. They took great risks economically and artistically in an era when few believed that studio furnituremaking was a meaningful movement in the field of the arts.

In the 1970s, a renewed interest in historical styles prompted artists and designers to freely adopt and adapt ideas from the past. Visual historicism became an integral part of new design practices. As a result, museum exhibitions made comparisons between old and new. But the similarities are often more the result of convergence than of influence. "Paint on Wood: Decorated American Furniture since the 17th Century," an exhibition mounted at the Renwick Gallery of the Smithsonian Institution in 1977, made comparisons between the old and new furniture on display, but no real links between past and present were established to give the exhibition intellectual cohesiveness.

In the 1980s many studio furnituremakers have eagerly examined historic furniture, probed its meaning, and incorporated it within their personal vocabularies. This revival of historical interest among the furnituremakers themselves prompted the staff of the Department of American Decorative Arts and Sculpture to explore works of the new generation. The resulting exhibition explores past and present tastes, where memory and imagination intersect. This seems to be the right moment to analyze real rather than virtual connections between historic and contemporary works, and to celebrate the fresh new attitudes about design, its history and process, shared by contemporary furnituremakers in America.

Jonathan L. Fairbanks
Katharine Lane Weems Curator of
American Decorative Arts and Sculpture

1. C. Dresser, *The Art of Decorative Design* (London: Day and Son, 1862) p. 107.
2. Owen Jones, *The Grammar of Ornament* (London: Day and Son, 1956), republished in 1986 by Studio Editions, London, argued against the slavish copying of antique ornamental motifs. For the most throrough analyses of this period, see *In Pursuit of Beauty: Americans and the Aesthetic Movement* (New York: The Metropolitan Museum of Art, 1987) and Wendy Kaplan, ed., *The Art that is Life: The Arts & Crafts Movement in America, 1875–1920* (Boston: Museum of Fine Arts, 1987).
3. Denman W. Ross. *A Theory of Pure Design: Harmony, Balance, Rhythm* (Boston and New York: Houghton Mifflin and Company, 1907). Pure design principles articulated by Ross were applied to practical problems by Charles Fabens Kelley and William Luther Mowell, *A Text Book of Design* (Boston, New York, and Chicago: Houghton Mifflin Company, 1912).
4. Ernest A. Batchelder, *Design in Theory and Practice* (New York: The Macmillan Company, 1910) p. vii.
5. For a summary of this period, see Karen Davies, *At Home in Manhattan: Modern Decorative Arts, 1925 to the Depression* (New Haven: Yale University Art Gallery, 1983).
6. Edwin Avery Park. *New Backgrounds For a New Age* (New York: Harcourt Brace and Company, 1927), pp. 15, 79.
7. T.H. Robsjohn-Gibbings. *Good-bye, Mr. Chippendale* 1944, p. 105.

ACKNOWLEDGMENTS

"New American Furniture" has been in the works for several years, and I have drawn upon the advice and assistance of many. The conceptual genesis of the exhibition occurred in the spring of 1982, when I was teaching "The American Craftsman in Historical Perspective" at Boston University and taking a woodworking course at the Program in Artisanry there. I began to recognize the interest of contemporary furnituremakers in historical furniture and the need to discuss the transformations in studio furnituremaking. Spurred on by the environment at BU, I developed an idea for the exhibition in which leading studio furnituremakers would draw inspiration from historical furniture. The inspiration could be a form, decorative detail, technical convention, or social use. Constant contact with the artists—visiting their studios, asking them to keep journals, developing a questionnaire, and talking with them frequently—would provide special insight into each individual's development and contribute valuable information for a broad discussion of the field and the specific analysis of a piece of furniture.

When I began to work at the Museum of Fine Arts in 1985, I immediately began planning the exhibition. Throughout the project Jonathan Fairbanks, Katharine Lane Weems Curator of American Decorative Arts and Sculpture, supported and encouraged the innovative approach to contemporary visual arts. I would also like to thank Alan Shestack, the Museum's director, for his support of a seemingly risky project in which there were no images of the work to be in the exhibition, only a concept and ideas.

To familiarize myself with the field and identify the invited furnituremakers, I combed magazines, attended shows, and was aided by the people I met at BU and several gallery owners. Judy Coady and Bernice Wollman of Workbench Gallery, Rick Snyderman of Snyderman Gallery, and Herta Loeser of the Society of Arts and Crafts were particularly helpful and shared their files and slides. To get the planning for the exhibition underway, the financial support of several parties with a knowledge of and interest in studio furniture provided an important catalyst. Among those who contributed to the planning expenses of "New American Furniture" were Ronald and Anne Abramson, Best Products Foundation, Dr. and Mrs. Joseph A Chazan, Patricia Conway, Hugh Hardy, Wallace F. Holladay, Jr., Peter T. Joseph, Roger M. Milgrim, and the Seminarians. Their enthusiasm, confidence, and financial assistance enabled us to bring twenty-six furnituremakers to the Museum of Fine Arts for a two-day symposium and to get the project off the ground. Their early support was critical in obtaining subsequent implementation support for the exhibition and catalogue from the National Endowment for the Arts.

My colleagues at the Museum greatly eased the tasks of organizing and writing. In the Department of American Decorative Arts and Sculpture, Maria Pulsone assisted with the voluminous correspondence and the movement of furniture to and from the photography studio. She, Linda Foss, Kathi Drummy, and Marti Hobbs cheerfully helped with data processing, ensuring efficient completion of the catalogue. Lauretta Dimmick and Jeannine Falino graciously assumed some of my day-to-day responsibilities, enabling me to better focus upon the project.

Janice Sorkow of the Photographic Services Department oversaw the photography of the pieces and provided enthusiastic support for the exhibition. John Woolf shot all the new furniture with great sensitivity for the work. Tom Lang and Bill Buckley of the Museum's studio took environmental portraits of several furnituremakers for the exhibition.

For the production of the catalogue, I greatly appreciated the skills and friendship of the Office of Publications. Cynthia Purvis edited the manuscript with an understanding of the material and with good humor, and Janet O'Donoghue designed a very clean and inviting publication.

Lisa Harris and Janet Spitz of the Development Office listened well to my ideas, helped me to formulate my ideas, and were instrumental in securing grant support for the implementation. Linda Thomas, Pat Loiko, Pam Delaney, Ann Dee, and Jill Kennedy of the Registrar's Office made the logistics of the exhibition smooth and always reacted enthusiastically to the furniture. Judith Downes and Susan Wong of the Design Department gave shape to my ideas for the installation and provided invaluable suggestions for organization and supplementary materials. Barbara Martin of the Department of Education provided helpful suggestions that made the exhibition labels and brochure clear and informative.

I have also drawn on colleagues from outside the Museum. Davira Taragin of the Detroit Institute of Arts read a draft of the essay and provided helpful insights; Jonathan Fairbanks, John Dunnigan, Alphonse Mattia, and Rosanne Somerson also read portions of the manuscript and provided invaluable comments. Franklin Parrasch provided encouragement and shared his knowledge of Dan Jackson. Nina Stritzler of the American Craft Museum helped me locate and acquire older photographs.

I would also like to thank all of the participating furnituremakers. They gave generously of their time, and their cooperation and collaboration eased the task of transporting work, gathering information, and writing biographies.

Finally I would like to thank my wife Carol and our children Ben and Rachel for patiently enduring the project and providing necessary relief and perspective.

Edward S. Cooke, Jr.

NEW AMERICAN FURNITURE:
SECOND-GENERATION STUDIO FURNITUREMAKERS

In the late 1980s, furniture has emerged as one of the most dynamic American visual arts, one in which art, design, and craft have converged. Increasingly, participants in each of these formerly distinct fields have drawn new ideas and vigor from the interplay or tension between three points of view: the idea and emotion of art, the form and concept of design, and the technique and materials of craft.[1] At a time when Modernism has lost its cultural hegemony and personal expression is replacing the abstract intellectualism of the past forty years, artists, architects, and craftspeople have broadened the concept of furniture, its style or expression, and the materials and techniques used in its production.[2] Whether explicit or implicit, the function of furniture makes it a very interactive genre: its form, decoration, imagery, materials, and workmanship evoke intellectual, emotional, and physical response.

The broadened conception of furniture has had particular impact on a group of college-educated craftspeople who have set up their own small shops to design and build custom work. These studio furnituremakers have mastered material and technique as a means to explore design, content, and imagery within the parameters of functional furniture.[3] Unified by their commitment to the primacy of design and the use of appropriate methods and materials, this group can be referred to as the "second generation" of American studio furnituremakers.

The term generation refers not to a strict age cohort, apprenticeship sequence, or stylistic progression, but rather to a group with a unifying philosophy. Furnituremakers active in the 1950s and 1960s were referred to as "first-generation craftsmen."[4] Ranging in age from Bill Keyser (b. 1936) to Wharton Esherick (b. 1887), and in educational background from Arthur Espenet Carpenter's and Walker Weed's liberal arts background to George Nakashima's architectural training, they were unified by an absolute reverence for wood and a tendency to design around the aesthetics of the material. Defining themselves as woodworkers, they emphasized material as an end unto itself.

Many of these first-generation woodworkers continued to work in the 1970s and 1980s, inspiring others to pursue furnituremaking as a career, but in a different vein. In the 1960s there was a limited effort to link furniture to sculpture and fine arts, emphasizing concepts and rejecting commonly held notions about function and technique. This effort, however, did not last long, or gain widespread support.

The furnituremakers who emerged in the 1970s gave equal attention to idea, form, and technique to create functional work layered with evocative or metaphorical meaning. No longer limited by the first generation's insistence on wood, preference for hand work, and singular notion of function, the new furnituremaker's primary concern is the cultural notion of furniture. The second generation incorporates a variety of materials and techniques to reinforce or contradict this cultural notion, and gives great attention to the process of design. The design process of the second generation resembles what the anthropologist Claude Levi-Strauss called *bricolage*. In the act of composition, the craftsperson breaks down existing forms and ideas into elemental parts, and combines or recasts these elements with a contemporary grammar to produce a new expression.[5]

THE 1950s—THE FIRST GENERATION OF STUDIO FURNITUREMAKERS

The American craft movement had roots in the design reforms of the late nineteenth and early twentieth centuries and the philanthropic-exploitative interest in regional vernacular culture of the 1920s and 1930s, but coalesced and matured in post–World War II prosperity, optimism, and nationalism.[6] An expanding economy, a release of pent-up consumerism, and increased advertising made people more aware of domestic furnishings and more able to purchase these goods.[7] At the same time, the demand for goods and general prosperity permitted some people to pursue alternative careers, to turn an avocation into a full-time commitment.

The growth of a consumerist culture and the increasing number of families able to buy houses ensured the extensive market for mass-produced factory furniture. The modern industrial style—characterized by simple clean design, evident industrial processes, reliance on modern industrial materials—and traditional colonial style—interpreted in very basic fashion and with inexpensive construction—became the staples of the American furniture factories. Tubular steel chairs and tables, modular storage units with steel framework, plank-seated Windsor-like chairs, drop-leaf tables with turned legs, and rudimentary bureaus remained the common choices.[8]

The high end of the furniture market featured three basic types: American industrial, imported Scandinavian, and custom-designed works.[9] The establishment of Cranbrook Academy of Art in the late 1920s had provided America with its own school for the interdisciplinary exploration of art and design. Although the original head of the school, Eliel Saarinen, favored a close designer-craftsperson collaboration, his son Eero and other designers who graduated from Cranbrook—Charles and Ray Eames, Florence Knoll, Harry Bertoia—extolled most of the Bauhaus philosophy, but found the dogmatic formalism of the Germans to be overbearing. The Cranbrook group and such contemporaries as George Nelson, unlike their Bauhaus mentors, used a variety of forms and materials to introduce expression and aesthetic value, even at the expense of a higher price or less apparent function. The Eames ottoman, Bertoia wire chair, and Eero Saarinen fiberglass chair are typical examples of the high-end aesthetic industrialism that emerged in the 1950s and gave American designers their international preeminence. Unlike the less expensive designs of Paul McCobb, however, these pieces of furniture were restricted to a wealthy clientele.[10]

A second type of high-end furniture in the late 1940s was Scandinavian imports. Even in the 1930s, Sweden and Denmark were mass-producing wood-based modern furniture in vernacular designs. By the late 1940s, the American demand for high-quality, competitively priced domestic furniture was being met by these direct forms with soft, gently curved lines executed in the warmth of wood with aesthetically pleasing joints. Many attributed the success of the Scandinavian furniture to the role of such cabinetmakers as Carl Malmsten, Hans Wegner, and Borge Morgensen in establishing designs and processes suitable for factory production. The interaction of cabinetmaker and industry resulted in furniture that combined the richness of hand-crafted work with the efficiency of mass-production.[11]

A third segment of the high-end market was the work of custom designer-craftsperson. Designers such as T. H. Robsjohn-Gibbings and Edward J. Wormley conceived of furniture that was modern in form, use, and materials, but that drew inspiration from a combination of colonial and Scandinavian prototypes. Such designers worked with both larger factories and smaller custom shops.[12]

Colonial revival and Scandinavian furniture also provided ideas for a related group of American woodworkers who had developed outside of the usual channels. Unlike other segments of the high end of the industry, these craftspeople neither grew up in the trade nor relied upon skilled immigrant labor. Executing their own designs in their own shops, these woodworkers provided an alternative to industrial design work. The two earliest and best-known examples of this group are Wharton Esherick and George Nakashima.[13]

Wharton Esherick had studied painting at the Philadelphia Museum School of Industrial Art and the Pennsylvania Academy of the Fine Arts in the first decade of the twentieth century, but only painted until the mid-1930s. Instead, he found himself drawn to woodcut printing and then to sculpture and furniture. Dissatisfied with available furniture and excited by the medium of wood, Esherick began to make furniture in the 1920s. His early furniture manifests an interest in surface decoration and carving combined with rudimentary joinery. By the early 1930s, Esherick was more concerned with form, and incorporated the geometry of cubism or the natural curved line of the material. However, Esherick's impact on American furniture during the 1930s and 1940s was minimal: much of his work was interior finish work and furniture for friends among the Main Line intellectual and cultural elite. Only when Esherick collaborated with Philadelphia architect George Howe on a room setting for the 1939 World's Fair did the furnituremaker gain the attention and interest of the national design field.

In the 1950s, Esherick began to produce more furniture, characterized by spare lines and shaped elements. He reacted, as he recalled later, against "the contemporary furniture being made—straight lines, sharp edges and right angles—and I conceived free angles and free forms; making the edge of my tables flow so that they would be attractive to feel or caress."[14] In spite of his intent to offer shaped wooden furniture instead of the rectilinear metal type offered by the industry, Esherick was still identified more with industrial design than with fine art, which in the 1950s began to withdraw into its own rarefied world. Don Wallance's influential *Shaping America's Products*, which examined the interaction of design and craftsmanship in American manufacture, included Esherick and Nakashima as two influential American designer-producers who worked in their own shops. The book also included Charles Eames as an example of an industrial design laboratory and the Herman Miller Company as an example of small-scale industry.[15]

George Nakashima's background was more typical of the period. Trained as an architect, Nakashima turned to furniture as a form of building in which he could involve himself "from beginning to end." He picked up basic woodworking skills while a member of an Aurobindo utopian community in the late 1930s and later when interned in a Japanese American relocation center during World War II. After his release, Nakashima moved to New Hope, Pennsylvania, and began producing simple furniture, predominantly tables and chairs. These works borrowed stylistically from American vernacular Windsor chairs and trestle tables, and conceptually from Japanese woodworking—especially its emphasis on simple lines and respect for wood. A third influence was Nakashima's architectural interest in engineering. With Nakashima's design sense and architectural experience, his one-man shop soon employed about a dozen people.

Esherick and Nakashima gained a foothold in the high-end custom furniture market after World War II primarily through their architectural connections, but their subsequent success was also closely linked to the emergence of the studio craft movement in the 1950s. In furniture, different aspects of this movement arose among the self-taught and within the educational system.

Amateur work had always been one mode of furniture production, but the possibilities for amateur work increased dramatically at the beginning of the twentieth century. The Arts and Crafts philosophy emphasized the importance of art or craft work in restoring balance to one's life. At the same time, a growing literature, including how-to books with plans, and inexpensive equipment enabled many to set up shops in their homes. This avocational spirit of craft remained strong through the 1940s and provided a foundation for new growth in the 1950s. At that time, economic prosperity and a reaction against mass-produced goods spurred some people to make craft a lifestyle and vocation.

Such liberal-arts majors as Art Carpenter and Walker Weed or such graphic designers as Sam Maloof turned their interests in furniture design and construction into new careers. These self-taught woodworkers began by making furniture for themselves, then for their friends and a slowly expanding circle of acquaintances. Marketing was primarily by word of mouth. A commitment to wood and a concern with the business of furnituremaking enabled these woodworkers to earn a living, but the greater reward was a sense of personal satisfaction.[16]

A second group of woodworkers emerged from a new training ground, the nation's colleges. The School for American Craftsmen (SAC), first established at Dartmouth College in 1944, was the first and most prominent college craft program to offer a major in woodworking and furniture design. The emphasis of the program was initially on "manual industry," a craft-based occupational therapy to rehabilitate disabled veterans. It was hoped that such training would give veterans employment while also raising the level of American design production. By 1946, when SAC was relocated to Alfred University, the program was no longer linked to therapy but rather to improving the craftsmanship of American production. Such a philosophical shift was not only a reaction against the flood of Scandinavian imports but also part of a national emphasis on and faith in college as the training ground for all careers. Art and design curricula grew and began to include craft courses. SAC offered majors in ceramics, metals, wood, and fiber. By 1946, SAC, like Cranbrook in the 1930s, sought to develop skilled graduates "who work not only as designers, modelmakers, foremen and artisans, but also as setters of fashion and styles and as experimenters in the use of materials and methods."[17] But SAC did not replicate Cranbrook's emphasis on architectural design. Instead of teaching academic industrial design, the program provided the students with the technical expertise to operate small self-sustaining shops. Although the Bauhaus-trained potter Frans Wildenhain was hired to teach ceramics, Danish-trained teachers dominated the faculty.

Tage Frid, who had apprenticed with a master cabinetmaker and had graduated from Copenhagen's School of Interior Design, was recruited in the spring of 1948 to teach furniture, thus linking the older European apprenticeship system and the new American school system.[18] Frid found that students were interested in "the freedom of the material," but had no interest in technique. His teaching therefore focused on knowledge of technique and wood technology, an emphasis that continued when the program moved to the Rochester Institute of Technology (RIT) in 1950. Because SAC was the only college-level program with a furniture major in the early 1950s, Frid's approach to design—construction determines form—exerted a singular influence on those who operated shops or began to teach in the 1960s.

Although those who took part in the revival of small-shop custom furniture included the self-taught, those trained in sculpture or architecture, and the university-educated, there was a certain stylistic coherence to the work of the 1950s. Most work demonstrated an affinity with the simple American vernacular, primarily Windsor chairs, Federal-period tables and case furniture, and Shaker furniture. Ironically, all of these were proto-industrial products whose parts could be produced in quantity and assembled as the need arose. A second stylistic strain was Scandinavian work, due both to Frid's background and the common cultural expression of the period. Studio craftsmen like Maloof and designers like Robsjohn-Gibbings produced works very similar to imports that appeared in the various periodicals of the same period.

Although the term *hand-crafted* has often been used to describe the work of these studio furnituremakers, the period literature quite explicitly refutes this notion. The craftsmen were not so tied to a romantic tradition that they unilaterally rejected the machine. Esherick, Maloof, and Frid recognized the positive aspects of machinery and emphasized its ability to save time, avoid drudgery, and ensure precision. Handwork complemented machine work and was used where it was most visible. Esherick declared,

"I use any damn machinery I can get hold of" to bring out the character of his wood. Only the lathe seems to have been rejected; its associations with industrial mill work may have been too great. Machined mortises and table-sawn tenons, however, were used in conjunction with sawn and chiseled dovetails, routed grooves, and shaper-contoured moldings. Maloof, for example, relied on routed joints secured with screws or dowels for his chair frames and casepieces, yet handcut the dovetails of drawers in individual pieces because it was more efficient than jigging them.[19]

While Frid emphasized the mastery of many techniques, there was little attempt to make precious or self-consciously decorated furniture. The technical range of the small shop was circumscribed by an overwhelming concern with material. The ultimate concern of the 1950s studio furnituremaker, as stated by Greta Daniel in *American Craft*, was "quiet refinement of contour and proportion, fine detailing, finishes, and particularly, a very personal choice of material." It was believed that the wood of a finished piece would clearly reveal the personality of its maker. Quiet, restrained use of solid wood, without interruption by carving or inlay, was considered sophisticated and effective. "It is frequently the withholding rather than the application of such decorations that shows virtue and understanding of one's material," Daniel wrote.[20] Esherick, who used curved lines to accentuate the grain of his boards and who allowed knots to project while sanding checks to accentuate them, extolled the vitality and intimacy of wood. Metal, he found, was "uncomfortable and too cold." Maloof spoke for his contemporaries when he remarked, "If you're working in wood, you just don't want to work in anything else. Why? Well, it's the warmth, the texture, the *feel* of wood . . . I don't need other materials."[21]

Although some of the period literature refers to those who worked in the 1950s as "designer-craftsmen," the term *designer* has a very specific meaning for that period. While the contemporary usage of the term implies an architectural, three-dimensional conception of form, designer-

craftspeople of the 1950s were decidedly anti-industrial and defined themselves by their rejection of mass-production. As a result, they emphasized wood and the intrinsic aesthetic value of each board: "Materials hold within themselves basic and inherent beauty. The task of the craftsman is first to know fully the character of his material. From such knowledge will come inspiration to incorporate the physical properties of his material as an intrinsic part of his design. Many materials need no decoration, for their qualities, well developed, are sufficient for great beauty."[22] The material basis of design is most clearly represented in the more common occupational label for the 1950s studio furnituremaker: woodworker. The absolute reverence for the material was taken to its ultimate level by Nakashima who referred to the soul of the tree and searched for the singular perfect use for each board.

The woodworkers of the 1950s sold their goods primarily to friends and increased their business through word of mouth. A crafts network did slowly evolve: craft fairs throughout the nation provided opportunities for the sale of smaller things, as did America House, a retail outlet in New York City run by the American Crafts Council (ACC). The cooperative Shop One in Rochester, New York, of which Frid was part-owner, was one of the few galleries to show furniture.

First-generation woodworkers were thus part of a national, pan-crafts community, the sum of which far exceeded the individual parts. In spite of a philosophy and commitment shared with craftspeople in other media, and nourished at the periodic ACC conferences in the late 1950s, woodworkers in the 1950s worked in relative isolation for a local or intimate clientele.

THE 1960s—THE CHALLENGE
OF ARTIST-CRAFTSPEOPLE

In the 1960s the new academic foundation of crafts removed those craftspeople who taught from direct dependence on the marketplace and opened up new opportunities. It encouraged interaction between crafts, fine arts, and design; provided the freedom and facilities to test new ideas; allowed stimulation from a constantly changing and questioning group of students; and provided visibility in shows at college and regional museums. Such an environment provided the catalyst for reaction against the emphasis on function and truth in materials that had so dominated in the 1950s, whether it resulted from traditionalism, industrial design, or Eastern craft philosophy. The leaders of the new revolution included Peter Voulkos, who taught ceramics at Otis Art Institute in Los Angeles, and Lenore Tawney, a fiber artist who studied and worked in New York. By adapting the principles of abstract expressionism to craft media, Voulkos and Tawney emphasized visual presence over function, form over material, and feeling over technique. Sculptural construction and painted or textured surfaces were typical ways to explore expressive content. Voulkos and Tawney began their new work in 1955, but it was not until the early 1960s that their ideas took hold in the field and in the schools.[23]

The emergence of new approaches in the early 1960s can be traced to both general and specific causes. The general American cultural attitude of that period was one of liberal exceptionalism—the openness of American society, the abundance of goods, and the intellectual vigor of the nation's art schools permitted American artists and craftspeople the freedom to experiment, take risks, and "make mistakes freely on a creative and quantitative level that is proportionally unequalled anywhere."[24] The boundaries of art were pushed into commercial art, advertising, design, and craft, and a rigorous intellectual dialogue between artist and critic accompanied the new work. Artists and craftspeople not only created new images and new objects, but

reinvested images and objects with value and power to create new attitudes. As a result, some craftspeople strove to explore the meaning of their work, incorporating themes of humor, wit, ritual, tragedy, and social criticism. More artists, on the other hand, took an interest in exploring the forms of their work by representing ordinary things.

Important to developments in the studio craft movement was the voice of Rose Slivka, a writer who was a close friend of Jackson Pollock, Franz Kline, and other members of the New York school of action painters. When she became editor of *Craft Horizons* in late 1959, Slivka steered the national publication away from the traditional interest in primitive art, lost techniques, and mainstream design, and introduced the work of Voulkos and others.[25]

In this shift in editorial philosophy, she emphasized that the new American craftsperson should not depend upon the past but have a sharp intellectual and aesthetic awareness of the present. Beginning in 1961, Slivka championed the cause of the new "freewheeling" work that broke new ground, challenged past traditions, and suggested new meanings and possibilities. To her, the work of Voulkos, Tawney, and others was "exuberant, bold, and irreverant," while more traditional work reflected a stifling emphasis on function and a lack of adventure.[26]

The exhibitions at the Museum of Contemporary Crafts in New York also reflected this polarized view. Whereas shows in the 1950s included "Young Americans and Young Scandinavians," "Tools, Techniques, and Materials," and "Finnish Rug Designs," the shows from the mid to late 1960s included "Woven Forms," "Fantasy Furniture," and "Objects are . . .?" The museum and *Craft Horizons* eagerly sought to elevate crafts to the status of fine art, but such aspirations did not go unchallenged. Many traditionalists were insulted by what they perceived as crude, grotesque, misshapen abominations. The new "textural adventure" violated accepted notions of pleasing design, appropriate use of materials, and standards of craftsmanship.[27]

While ceramics and fiber permitted ecumenical

inclusion of a range of artist-craftspeople from traditional weavers or potters to avant-garde sculptors, the world of wood was fragmented in the early 1960s. Some of those who worked in wood hived off into the world of sculpture. H. C. Westermann, who had worked as a carpenter while studying fine arts at the School of The Art Institute of Chicago, began to apply his knowledge of wood and wood technology to conceptual sculpture in the late 1950s and early 1960s. Unlike more traditional sculptors who used such subtractive techniques as carving and modeling, Westermann took a more constructional approach in which he chose particular types of woods, assembled them with appropriate carpentry or joinery techniques, and finished the piece with handtools and traditional oil finishes. He used this carpenter's approach to explore direct, visceral themes of existentialism. While he used basic wood techniques, though, Westermann did not view the wood or the related techniques as ends unto themselves as did the contemporary woodworkers: "Craftsmanship is very secondary actually. I like the quality of idea first. . . . Craftsmanship is only, you know, to serve a purpose, other purposes." Westermann used the material and its attendant technologies to explore themes of humor or despair, but never attempted to perfect his technical knowledge. Instead he consciously nurtured the *effect of woodworking* with large screws or dovetails or even inlaid knots or checks.[28]

Another woodworker who opted for the gallery world of contemporary art in the early 1960s was Richard Artschwager. He had earned a living as a woodworker in the late 1950s, even showing a typical Scandinavian-inspired desk at the 1957 Museum of Contemporary Crafts exhibition entitled "Furniture by Craftsmen," but began in the early 1960s to react against the confining reverence for wood characteristic of studio furniture in the 1950s. Artschwager attacked the deeply ingrained notions of wood and function by using Formica to build pieces of furniture that merely represented furniture. Artschwager grew "sick of looking at all this beautiful wood" that he had stocked in his shop and found that it evoked only a negative reaction. It was no

longer inherently beautiful. Instead he discovered Formica, "the great ugly material, the horror of the age." Artschwager was attracted by the commonness and representational qualities of Formica and began to use it to build pictures of furniture that explored the image or function of the form.[29]

Few woodworkers, however, paid attention to the paths explored by Westermann and Artschwager. The two main figures of the 1960s who sought to move beyond woodworking and make artistic furniture were Wendell Castle and Tommy Simpson, both of whom showed work in the 1966 Museum of Contemporary Crafts exhibition "Fantasy Furniture."[30] Castle, trained in industrial design and sculpture, began to make furniture in 1958 and soon rejected traditional forms and techniques. He expressed disdain for the rectilinear furniture of the past and emphasized the need for original, organic forms. To build this new furniture, Castle borrowed stack lamination techniques from sculpture and became the first woodworker to use this technique as the sole construction method in making functional furniture.

Castle's anti-historical approach and commitment to adapting sculptural techniques to emphasize form rather than technique influenced a number of woodworkers in the late 1960s and 1970s. In spite of their interest in new forms and techniques, Castle and his followers continued the first generation's reverence for wood. The canon of material was not really challenged. Although Esherick and others of the first generation did not view Castle as a woodworker—Esherick felt that Castle was only after form and that he lacked respect for wood's beauty—Castle's forms do emphasize the natural qualities of wood, even if they were created artificially.[31]

Tommy Simpson more completely rejected the heritage of the 1950s. Trained as a painter at the Cranbrook Academy of Art, Simpson combined his interest in paint and painting techniques with his deep attachment to domestic furnishings as affecting presences, capable not only of functioning as seating or storage forms, but also of telling stories, evoking humor or grief, or providing a sense of place in history. For Simpson, in the 1960s, technique was merely a means to achieve the desired imagery and wood was merely a convenient medium. He would glue and peg together inexpensive woods like yellow poplar and pine to construct very anthropomorphic shapes and then heavily paint them with acrylics to make his intent more obvious. The technique and painting style worked well together. As Simpson later explained: "To make them clumsy makes them more childlike—they fit my theme of whimsy better. Too much craftsmanship seems too educated. I make them this way intentionally."[32]

In spite of its relationship to work in other media, Simpson's furniture at this time did not really attract the attention accorded to fiber and ceramics by the avant-garde craft world. The decentralized nature of woodworking, the limited opportunities for exhibition, and the longer and broader roots of ceramics and fiber in the academic system all worked against the inclusion of woodworking in contemporary art. In the 1960s most woodworkers worked from order to order, trying to drum up business, and occasionally putting work in the growing number of small regional or university museum exhibitions. The cost of shipping large and heavy furniture severely restricted the inclusion of furniture in most of these low-budget shows. Ceramics and fiber, because they could be shipped more easily, dominated these shows.[33] Only Castle demonstrated a keen interest in taking risks, consistently placing his work in such shows.

RIT remained the only college-level furniture program until 1962, when the Rhode Island School of Design established a furniture program and hired Tage Frid away from RIT. Although Castle replaced Frid at RIT, Frid's influence remained strong, in part because Castle's assistant, Bill Keyser, was a former student of Frid's. As the senior professor, Frid had a profound impact upon the direction of academic furnituremaking. He instilled a strong technical foundation, at the expense of design and creativity. The inertia of his singular dominance was difficult to overcome. Not until some of his former students

began to teach in other furniture programs at other institutions in the 1960s and 1970s did there develop a critical dialogue that gave more weight to design and idea.

Two of Frid's students played particularly important roles: Jere Osgood and Dan Jackson. Both came to RIT with considerable talent and learned a great deal from Frid, but sought to pursue more creative work. Osgood had a strong design background. His architectural training at the Illinois Institute of Technology had developed his sense of architectural history and his drafting skills, and he had been trained to systematically work through a design program, develop designs from ideas and existing designs, and integrate concept, technique, and form. Osgood's architectural perspective merged with Frid's technical emphasis to produce a more balanced integration of design and wood.[34]

Jackson had worked as an antiques restorer before matriculating to RIT. He profited greatly from Frid's technical instruction and Osgood's friendship, but the most meaningful part of his education was the two years he spent in Copenhagen, from 1960 to 1962. There he worked with Peder Moos, a skilled cabinetmaker who was exploring new decorative versions of the Danish modern styles. Moos retained the structural and technical basis of Danish furniture, but explored the effect of shaping and lightening members without sacrificing structural strength or compromising cabinetmaking techniques.[35]

In the early and mid 1960s, Osgood and Jackson struggled to develop their new notions. Osgood supported himself by making small accessories to be sold through America House while developing new designs and techniques to lighten the structure of his furniture and to introduce more sophisticated curved lines. Underlying Osgood's interest in curves was his interest in the intrinsic properties of wood: he believed that wood should move and curve more than it had in Frid's work of the 1950s, but that the craftsperson should not violate and waste the wood by removing it to make organic forms as Castle had done. Instead Osgood emphasized preplanning and the development of jigs to use and shape the wood economically and sensitively. Toward this end, he developed two techniques in the late 1960s, tapered lamination, used primarily for legs, and compound bent-stave lamination for carcasses.

Jackson started to find his own niche in 1964 when he was hired to teach three-dimensional design and head the new furniture department at the Philadelphia College of Art (PCA). PCA students spent their first two years getting a broad foundation in a variety of two- and three-dimensional media and only concentrated on a major medium in their junior year. Jackson found this the ideal environment in which to explore Moos's ideas as well as his own conceptual ones, especially the pyscho-sexual imagery of the period. In regard to technique and form, Jackson encouraged the use of visible joinery and the shaping or paring away of material in the structural elements. Most woodworkers at that time used mitered corners, dovetailed drawers, lap joints, and through-morticed joints, but often tried to downplay their effect. Jackson, on the other hand, liked to contrast end grain and face grain by using several of the common joints as well as dovetailed bridle joints. He emphasized the importance of traditional construction techniques and the value of an additive approach to carving, wherein carved ornament gracefully related the joined parts.

To get students to think broadly about concept and design, Jackson not only showed slides or pictures of furniture—from antique to Art Nouveau to Scandinavian Modern—but also talked about Westermann's work, drew ideas from such popular culture as comic books, and consistently argued the need for more adventurous and conceptual designs in wood. But he always emphasized function: "There is not a great difference between the two (sculpture and furniture). Furniture must fill a specific function. Then it can go on to be aesthetic. Sculpture is purely aesthetic from the beginning. What I am trying to do is marry the two." Charismatic, intense, passionate, and provocative, Jackson was an inspiring teacher. In his teaching and his work, he was intuitive and impulsive, but at the same time analytical and exacting.

Jackson also served as a catalyst for the entire Phila-delphia craft art community. He interacted with the metal and glass programs at PCA, attracted the attention of gallery owners like Helen Drutt, and helped to establish the Triannual Philadelphia Craftsman show. By the late 1960s Philadelphia was the center not only of studio furniture but of studio crafts in general.

The state of the studio furniture field in the 1960s is best summed up in two important exhibitions, "Woodenworks" and "Objects USA."[36] Although the former opened in 1972, much of the work dated from the 1950s and 1960s and manifests the strength of the first generation's canon of material. The exhibition focused on the work of five masters: Wharton Esherick, George Nakashima, Sam Maloof, Art Carpenter, and Wendell Castle. Only Castle possessed a radical voice in this exhibition, yet his work of the 1960s shared the same wood emphasis of the others. In addition, Castle's work in the show dated prior to 1969, when he began to paint some work and then rejected wood in order to explore his ideas and forms in painted fiberglass. Yet while "Woodenworks" looked backwards at the studio furniture movement, it still brought the work to the attention of a broader, more national audience.

"Objects USA," a traveling exhibition organized in 1969 by New York gallery owner Lee Nordness and funded by S.C. Johnson and Son, celebrated American craft of the 1960s and also helped to familiarize the public with the studio craft movement. While ceramics and fiber dominated the exhibition, furniture was well represented. Although Maloof, Nakashima and Esherick were featured prominently, Nordness also included Castle's more current fiberglass work, Simpson's painted work, and a chest of compound bent-stave lamination by Osgood. "Objects USA" thus demonstrated the domination of the first-generation woodworkers, the isolated alternatives of the 1960s, and the future direction of the 1970s.

1970s—THE EMERGENCE OF THE SECOND GENERATION

At the same time that "Woodenworks" brought woodworking of the 1950s and 1960s to the public eye, the field itself began to develop in a different direction in the 1970s. Castle's anti-historical organic style and simple techniques inspired many woodworkers and spawned imitators; stack lamination became synonymous with contemporary popular American furniture of the 1970s. Some woodworkers in England and Europe viewed this freeing technique as an important contribution to furniture design. But many, including Castle himself, had doubts about the technique and its related organic forms: the noticeable lines of the laminated joints proved distracting and compromised the aesthetic unity of the furniture, the forms looked too massive, and the techniques wasted a great deal of material.[37]

In order to quell his doubts, Castle temporarily abandoned woodworking between 1969 and 1973 in order to make hand-built plastic furniture. This venture proved unsuccessful, and Castle returned to wood, making chairs based on industrial designs of the mid-twentieth century, desks and seating furniture in his 1960s stack-laminated style, and tables in a more historical manner. While supporting himself with this work, Castle searched for a new way to gain acceptance in the fine art galleries of New York. In 1976, Castle began to make illusionistic objects that consisted of traditional furniture forms, on which he displayed everyday objects carved in wood. This *trompe l'oeil* work received attention from both craft and art critics in the late 1970s, leading to a one-person show at Carl Solway's gallery in New York. While this show was not commercially successful, a single piece of the *trompe l'oeil* sold within the next few years at a record price for contemporary furniture.[38]

Castle's *trompe l'oeil* work, however, had a greater impact upon the studio-furniture market than on the furniture itself. Castle's earlier dislike of traditional furniture design, disdain for technical conventions, and emphasis on

form had stimulated oppositional voices. Frid at RISD continued to argue that technique and a concern for the movement of wood should determine design. But it was James Krenov, an American-born, Swedish-trained woodworker, who became the philosophical conscience of the 1970s. Krenov exerted an influence not in his work, but in his writings and lectures. He criticized the 1950s emphasis on material at the expense of craftsmanship, and lashed out against insensitive treatment of wood and the heavy-handed design of the sculptural stack-laminated work of the 1960s and 1970s. Krenov felt that, without a proper balance of knowledge and skill, too much emotion or egoism resulted in "contrived, artsy furniture" that pandered to the marketplace. Although faulted for his personal and dogmatic view and criticized for his unadventurous designs, Krenov's call for balancing the emphasis on technique and material and the interest in design and concept was well received by the growing number of college-trained furnituremakers in the 1970s.[39]

While Krenov provided some of the philosophical underpinnings for a new direction, Jackson and Osgood provided the actual leadership and should be recognized as the leaders of the second generation of studio furnituremakers. The former's inspired teaching and the latter's commitment to design and appropriate technique had an immense impact. Together they began to push the field beyond an ultimate concern with wood and to uphold high standards of both conception and construction. Their influence can be seen most clearly in the programs with which they were associated.

Two of Jackson's students at PCA in the late 1960s gave shape to their teacher's vision. Ed Zucca, a 1968 graduate, worked initially in an organic, heavily carved style. But in 1972 his emphasis shifted from material to design. He recognized that the accentuation of wood's inherent beauty often detracted from the design or concept of a piece. Rather than reject his knowledge of woodworking techniques, he used his training in furniture construction as a foundation and developed into a designer who worked confidently and competently in wood. Zucca used the medium to set up playful or ironic statements. For example, he juxtaposed traditional and futuristic connotations by building a high-tech table out of wood and with wood joints, and then sealed the wood and sprayed it with metallic paint. On other work, he painted wood to resemble stone, used light emitting diodes as inlays, and drew from a variety of influences ranging from ancient Egyptian motifs, Shaker forms, Mayan architecture, toys, and the work of H.C. Westermann. Within all his work, Zucca maintained Jackson's emphasis on achieving balance between function, solid technique, and aesthetic content.[40]

Alphonse Mattia, who graduated from PCA in 1969, also worked in a somewhat organic manner at first. His interest in teaching, however, led him to study with Frid at RISD, where he received an M.F.A. in 1973. In the late 1970s, he began to merge Jackson's conceptual emphasis and Frid's technical mastery to explore fantasy, memory, emotion, and representational elements. His work related to function, but explicit utility was not always the end result. Equally valid to Mattia was the use of familiar parts to create something new. At the end of the 1970s Mattia also introduced more color through paint, varieties of wood, and dyed veneers, in an effort to overturn the material limitations that had dominated the field since the 1950s.[41]

Unlike Simpson and Castle in the 1960s, who had simply covered up their solid wood armatures with paint, both Mattia and Zucca used paint as an integral part of design and construction. Paint was only one possibility in their repertoire, a repertoire characterized by a far greater breadth than that of a 1950s woodworker.

Jackson also played a significant role in setting up Boston University's Program in Artisanry (PIA), founded in 1975.[42] Although James Krenov was hired to head the program and give it immediate stature, he left after teaching only the first semester, in the spring of 1975. Jere Osgood, who had been hired as a part-time assistant, suddenly found himself the only teacher for the new pro-gram. Osgood, who had known Jackson since 1959 and had taught at PCA during Jackson's 1971 sabbatical, suggested that PIA director Neil Hoffman invite Dan Jackson to help Osgood establish the new program. Although illness had diminished Jackson's own technical prowess, his intensity, demanding questions, and charisma provided the program with its academic edge. Discussions of ideas, sketch reviews, and visualization exercises emphasized the importance of design, while technical exercises fostered a familiarity with wood and encouraged the exploration of appropriate techniques. Instead of following Frid's maxim—"design around construction"—PIA students were taught to construct around design and were offered a wide variety of ideas to envision the design and a broad selection of technical approaches to execute it.

Jackson and Osgood also developed a degree structure to attract a diverse group of skilled furnituremakers. The program offered standard Associate's or Bachelor's degrees in furniture design but also encouraged accomplished cabinetmakers to pursue a Certificate of Mastery, a non-degree award. Such a structure permitted the matriculation of established cabinetmakers like Bruce Beeken, Tim Philbrick, and Richard Tannen, all of whom were seeking a broader and freer approach to design without the burden of a regular college curriculum. PIA's stimulating atmosphere expanded their horizons, and they in return contributed their own experiences and approaches to fellow students and teachers.

The Osgood-Jackson team provided ideal leadership: Osgood's engineering and design skills and self-effacing personality provided both a firm foundation and a freedom based on this security, and Jackson's ecumenical interest in artistic expression and ability to push students in new directions gave the students the means to build on Osgood's philosophy. In the academic year 1975–1976, Jackson provided the spirit and voice of the program, while Osgood oversaw its daily rhythms and technical instruction. While Jackson's declining health forced his retirement after one year, Jackson's successor, Alphonse Mattia, maintained the imaginative spirit Jackson had established at PIA.

The art historian John Kirk, an authority in early American furniture, also played an invaluable role in the PIA program. Kirk's expertise in American historical work, his previous training as a cabinetmaker at RIT and as a furniture designer at the Royal Danish Academy of Fine Arts, and his familiarity with both colonial and contemporary work made the past more accessible to the PIA students. Kirk used the collections of the Museum of Fine Arts and other nearby institutions not only to provide students with a solid base in historical furniture styles and construction, but also to force them to develop a critical eye that would record details and evaluate designs.

The students at PIA were thus exposed to a wide variety of ideas and precedents, from seventeenth-century turned chairs to color-field painting, from Chippendale's *Cabinetmaker's Director* to television, from hand-chopped mortices to biscuit joints. Ideas and techniques were varied, but the commitment to forethought, planning, and engineered construction was uncompromising. Parts or images from the past or contemporary culture like Tim Philbrick's use of Federal forms and Alphonse Mattia's use of paint were not merely grafted upon existing forms, but were incorporated in the very conception of the final product. Both Philbrick and Mattia began their personal explorations in the mid 1970s and thus paralleled similar efforts by architects. Philbrick's neoclassical forms were very specific, personal responses to the cultural environment and had their roots in his earlier restoration work rather than in the popular Post-Modernist architecture. Mattia painted some of his work, using realism, texturalism, and pattern to add layers of irony or imagery to his work.

From 1976 until 1985, when Boston University closed PIA, the teaching partnership of Osgood and Mattia attracted top-notch students, inspired a new body of functional and expressive work, and dramatically shaped the field and the marketplace. The camaraderie among teachers and students at PIA bred confidence and provided support. The emphasis on making a living by selling studio furniture

distinguished the 1970s PIA approach from the 1960s PCA approach, which emphasized the creation of art rather than the living by creating, and the 1950s RIT approach, which emphasized the working of wood. PIA students thus graduated with a greater sense of professional commitment, and most have remained active in the making of furniture.

While PIA represents the pinnacle of creative energy during the late 1970s, it was also part of a broader interest in furniture. The tactile qualities of the objects in the "Woodenworks" show, the passionate writings of Krenov, and a more formal cultural environment brought changes to all levels of the field. Such self-taught furnituremakers as Garry Knox Bennett and John Dunnigan no longer followed the conservative "wood for wood's sake" approach. In the mid-1970s Bennett began to explore the formal possibilities of wood in conjunction with the decorative possibilities of metal, and Dunnigan used his close study of ancient Egypt, Greece, and Italy to develop his own academic classicism. Both the marriage of wood and metal and the historical approach would have been impossible in the organicism of the 1960s or the woodiness of the 1950s.

Vitality and professionalism also characterized the academic portion of the field. Enrollment increased in the established furniture design and construction programs at RIT, RISD, San Diego State University, and Virginia Commonwealth University. Even students in these more conservative programs, such as Rick Wrigley at RIT and Hank Gilpin at RISD, began to participate in the newer energy. Graduates from these schools also staffed new furniture programs at such smaller colleges as Bucks County Community College and Indiana University of Pennsylvania, and such craft schools as Penland School and Haystack Mountain School of Crafts. Alternative training programs such as David Powell's Leeds Design Workshop in Easthampton, Massachusetts; Ian Kirby's Hoosuck Design and Woodworking in North Adams, Massachusetts; and the Wendell Castle Workshop in Scottsville, New York, also emerged in the last half of the decade.[43] The increased activity of individuals and schools signalled the maturity of studio furnituremaking.

In the 1970s more women sought to become professional furnituremakers. In the past, social or cultural restrictions had prevented women from really entering the male domain of furniture making. Some widows of cabinetmakers in the colonial period had overseen the shops of their deceased husbands, but most of the decisions and activity remained in the shop where the pieceworkers, journeyman, or apprentices carried on. In the late nineteenth century, women's artistic talents were applied to the carving or decoration of furniture, but the design and construction remained men's work. The shift to college training for craftspeople after World War II opened up the possibilities for women to pursue furnituremaking careers, but it was the feminism of the early 1970s that prompted an appreciable number of women to enter the school programs. By the late 1970s a number of successful and prominent female furnituremakers—Judy Kensley McKie, Rosanne Somerson, and Wendy Maruyama among them—had broken down gender barriers and become role models. McKie's sculptural work attracted considerable critical attention, Somerson became an influential writer and educator, Maruyama and Gail Friedell Smith earned M.F.A.s in furniture from RIT in 1980. All have played major roles in determining the direction of furnituremaking.[44]

In spite of the growing number of furnituremakers and furniture programs, the status of the studio furnituremaker remained problematic. Hard work and a focus upon the domestic market had enabled such first-generation craftspeople as Sam Maloof, Art Carpenter, and George Nakashima to make a living solely from their furniture, but recognition came only after they had struggled for many years. Few of those who began working in the 1960s and 1970s lived solely by making furniture. Tommy Simpson, Ed Zucca, Hank Gilpin, and Judy McKie are among the few second-generation furniture makers who struggled to make a living without teaching, although Simpson and Zucca have served as guest instructors on occasion. Wendell Castle, Jere Osgood, and Dan Jackson all taught not only to spread their new approaches and stimulate their own ideas, but also to support themselves, since their work was not always targeted for the consumer. Less familiar and overtly functional than the work of the first generation, their experimental work was labor intensive and was often made speculatively for an exhibition.[45]

The increase in the numbers of furnituremakers was accompanied by a related increase in the demand for studio furniture. More qualified furnituremakers resulted in more work, but the development of the market was closely connected to increased visibility, especially in galleries and museums. In Philadelphia, the center of studio furniture, woodworker Richard Kagan opened the first gallery devoted exclusively to wood and furniture in 1973. Kagan showed a wide variety of work, from the conservative older approaches of the turner Bob Stocksdale, to the organic work of Wendell Castle, to the newer refined works of Dan Jackson, Jere Osgood, Ed Zucca, Alphonse Mattia and other emerging students at PCA, RISD, RIT, and PIA. The Richard Kagan Gallery gave furnituremakers hope that their work could be successful both artistically and commercially.[46]

Studio furniture also received public recognition in museums. Small regional museums mounted many invitational and juried exhibitions in the 1970s. The "Please Be Seated" program at the Museum of Fine Arts, Boston, introduced many to the tactile and aesthetic joys of studio furniture. In 1975 the museum's curator of American decorative arts and sculpture, Jonathan Fairbanks, began to match National Endowment for the Arts funds with private or corporate gifts to commission contemporary public seating in the Museum's galleries. The first commission, in 1976, of fourteen pieces of seating furniture made by Sam Maloof was followed three years later by the work of Tage Frid, George Nakashima, Wendell Castle, and Judy McKie. In 1977, Fairbanks organized "Contemporary Works by Master Craftsmen," a small exhibition featuring the work of Sam Maloof, Wendell Castle, Tage Frid, Jere Osgood,

Alphonse Mattia, Bill Keyser, and Mark Singer as well as potters Rick Hirsch and Bill Wyman, metalsmith Albert Paley, jewelers Fred Woell and Robert Ebendorf, and glassblower Mark Peiser.[47]

Two exhibitions at the Museum of Contemporary Crafts in New York in the late 1970s demonstrate further the rise of furniture in the crafts hierarchy. A 1977 exhibition of fiber, wood, leather, and plastics made by artist-craftspeople under the age of thirty, entitled "Young Americans," featured twenty-two furnituremakers out of a total of ninety-five participants.[48] But the extensive press coverage given "New Handmade Furniture," the inaugural show at the newly named American Craft Museum, provides the clearest evidence of the intense interest in the studio furniture movement. The 1979 exhibition also reveals the changing composition of the field. It included familiar Maloof work, stack-laminated work by Wendell Castle and others who followed his lead, sculptural work by Judy Kensley McKie and John McNaughton, and the refined joinery of Jere Osgood and PIA graduates Michael Hurwitz and Thomas Hucker.[49]

"New Handmade Furniture" trumpeted the maturity of the studio furniture field and revealed the impact of PIA, but another harbinger of change in 1979 was the work of Garry Knox Bennett, an irreverent California soul in the spirit of Peter Voulkos. Trained as a metalworker and sculptor, Bennett in the late 1970s found himself drawn increasingly to wood as a medium with which he could make large objects fairly quickly. As he refined his woodworking skills, he grew dissatisfied with the confining sentimentality for wood and the emphasis on technique. To articulate his frustration, he built a sleek display cabinet of padouk—replete with tight joints, bent lamination, and sophisticated hardware—then randomly drove a bent 16p nail into a door on the front facade and surrounded the nail with a series of hammer impressions. Featured on the back cover of *Fine Woodworking* in the fall of 1980 along with a desk by Wendy Maruyama that had scribbled crayon decoration on its writing surface, Bennett's cabinet elicited the same response that Voulkos's ceramics had in the late 1950s. Traditionalists decried the "desecration" of the object and bemoaned the loss of standards, but the cabinet provided a single powerful image of the new interest in content and the recognition that sophisticated joinery and reverence for materials were not ends unto themselves.[50] The ideas behind Bennett's work fused with those behind the historically based work of Dunnigan and Philbrick and those behind the new PIA work to set the second-generation furniture makers on course for the 1980s.

1980s—THE DOMINANCE OF THE SECOND GENERATION

The late 1970s and early 1980s proved advantageous to the second-generation studio furnituremaker, who had successfully combined a solid foundation in traditional techniques and high-quality workmanship with an open-minded emphasis on concept and design. Broad-based efforts were being made in art, architecture, design, music, and literature to overturn the abstraction of Modernism and restore contextual meaning to artistic expression. While these efforts have often been lumped together under the rubric of Post-Modernism, the current narrow stylistic meaning of that term has blurred the various impulses for reform.

Of primary importance in art was Modernism's crisis of certainty. The need to constantly invent an avant-garde position had become self-absorbed, circular, and, therefore, alienated from normal activity. Instead of pursuing a constant dialectic for radical criticism and renewal in a Marxist manner, artists and critics began to explore a less confrontational sort of cumulative formation, one that incorporated the past rather than rejected it and explored technique and materials rather than denying them. Innovation and change became more appropriate and accessible by means of a dialogue with the past. New work could, therefore, become better understood. Artists no longer linked conceptual integrity with dispassionate feeling or dematerialization, but rather explored concept with a wider range of explicit emotions and with greater sensitivity to materials and techniques.[51]

Architects also began to question the Modernist emphasis on pure form and explicit function. Instead of viewing ornament as eclectic historicism that is merely applied, architects began to recognize that ornament could be integrated into the meaning of the structure and serve as an important component in its symbolic dimension. In *Complexity and Contradiction in Architecture* (1966), Robert Venturi articulated the first critique of Modernism's disdain for ornament. Venturi pointed out that ornament and style were not absolute entities, frozen in time with constant appearances and meanings, but possessed a variety of everchanging associative levels or codes, some of which were ambiguous or contradictory. The complexity of meanings provided decorated structures with a richness that engaged the viewer or user and resulted in an emotional and intellectual exercise different from the cerebral effect of Modernism. In *Complexity and Contradiction* and a second book, *Learning from Las Vegas*, Venturi emphasized the need to draw ideas and inspiration from the varieties of classical and popular cultural expression.[52]

By the late 1970s, many other architects had embraced Venturi's point of view, and used classical and vernacular forms and decoration to provide iconographic vitality and emotional meaning. The best of such work did not merely apply architectonic quotations to existing forms, but rather reinterpreted the past in the process of composition, thereby integrating ornament and structure. The resulting work manifested a link with design tradition, yet remained timely and contemporary.

The effect of new conceptual directions can also be noted in the marketplace for home furnishings. In the 1950s and 1960s most people purchased mass-produced, standardized objects that were restyled every few years in an effort to stimulate consumption. The various manifestations of the Modern style, Good Design, or Pop furnishings were the perfect product for these passive consumers. In the 1970s, however, consumers began to play a more active

role, and some makers of domestic goods offered more individualistic, distinctive objects designed to appeal to more materialistic users and buyers. As Victor Margolin described it, "design for consumption" gave way to "design for use."[53] To humanize design and endow objects with more intellectually and emotionally affecting presences, small firms and individuals explored and experimented with the juxtaposition of old and new materials, color, texture, and ornament.

The Italian critique against Modernist design gained the greatest popular recognition from 1979 to 1982. Architects and designers associated with Studio Alchymia, especially Ettore Sottsass and Andrea Branzi, challenged the expressive poverty and presumptive arrogance of Modernist aesthetics by recasting design as a form of non-verbal communication that depended upon decorative appearance for meaning. Their furniture was made with such industrial materials as plastic laminates, sheet metal, and neon, but these materials were integrated or juxtaposed with more traditional materials to create new contexts and relationships. This material exploration, along with an emphasis on color and compositional sense based upon the assemblage of decorated units, became the trademark of Alchymia and its more noted successor, the Memphis Group. Unlike the former's emphasis on experimental prototypes, the latter was distinguished by its commitment to industrial materials and factory production and by its enormous impact on international design from 1981 to 1983.[54]

Because designers have such an important position in the hierarchy of the Italian furniture industry—nearly all firms regardless of size depend upon architects and designers—the Memphis designers were able to produce quickly a large number of New Design pieces to show throughout the world. Yet while this New Design extended certain intellectual and aesthetic parameters, it did not challenge the basic structure of Modernist furniture production. Implicit within New Design was an emphasis on immediate excitement, a disregard for lasting quality workmanship, and an expectation of continuing design obsolescence. As New

Design subsumed Pop work, the vocabulary of the language changed, but much of the grammar and syntax did not. Like bean bag chairs and disposable furniture of the 1960s, the Memphis work remained "semi-works of art," whose color, iconoclastic forms, and sculptured shapes were intended to communicate a hip lifestyle.[55]

In America, the reaction against Modern furniture design was not as constrained as in Italy since its design and production was not so centralized within a rigid design hierarchy. Although architects and designers have worked with the furniture industry to produce work much like Italian New Design, studio furnituremakers, artists, and sculptors have produced work that not only overturns Modern aesthetics, but also embodies greater concern for individual expression and long lasting effect. Not committed by machinery, labor costs, and marketing to a narrow line of products, American studio craftspeople and artists have taken chances and explored new variations in an aggressive effort at combining art and design. Instead of emphasizing abstract design, functional art reaffirms the humanizing elements that combine emotion and intellect: the object's stance, the change in its appearance as one approaches, its feel and use, the level of physical or psychological comfort it affords, and the quality of its workmanship. Furnituremakers, in particular, have embraced a wide variety of responses—symbolic or metaphoric utility to traditional styling—in order to make objects more expressive.[56]

The independence from industry of studio furnituremakers affords them the freedom, unavailable to practitioners of Italian New Design, to select their own materials and to change or refine a design in process. The result has been more richness, excitement, or ambiguity. But unlike the first-generation woodworker, the second-generation studio furnituremaker uses technique and material merely as a means. In 1983, the Oakland furnituremaker Gail Friedell Smith had warned "While technical proficiency is a means to freedom of creative thought and work, it is not necessarily a prerequisite for creativity nor does it guarantee success. Woodworking will not come of age until woodworkers stop thinking of technique and wood as ends unto themselves, and start producing pieces of aesthetic value and conceptual substance."[57] Such a transformation was taking place as Smith wrote, primarily due to the large number of college-trained furnituremakers who probed understanding and meaning in their work and who argued that technique was no longer enough.

Furnituremakers continue to emphasize technical excellence and workmanship as an integral part of their visually rich and powerful work, but look to concept, new materials, and broader use of wood. Conceptually, they embrace the challenge of utility, often narrowly defining it or presenting it unconventionally—Michael Pierschalla's table, for example, has a top so small as to be almost imaginary, and Mattia's valet chairs have a very narrow range of functional uses but a very broad range of visual uses. They often play off literal and figurative meanings, as does Tommy Simpson in his quintessential rocking chairs—a mixture of early American Windsor chairs and late nineteenth-century porch rockers, replete with carved and painted symbols of nostalgia and historical memory—or Ed Zucca in his Shaker television set—a three-dimensional oxymoron constructed with Shaker-inspired lines and techniques and embellished with a Shaker tape speaker grill and zebrawood screen.

While wood has remained popular for its warmth, workability, and immediacy, the material has been treated less reverently and rigidly. Second-generation furnituremakers increased their technical repertoires by using such industrial machines as lathes, which had been shunned by first-generation woodworkers, and accepting such new technologies as plate-biscuit joinery, a spline-based joining system ideal for making large, awkward joints and complex angles.[58] The first generation's dictates—never obscure the beauty of wood, design to serve it, and work to enhance it—have been replaced by an interest in mixing wood with aluminum or bronze, stone, blown or cast glass, stone or concrete, plastic, specially designed textiles, or found materials. Even when wood is used, it is often colored with automobile enamel, milk paint, or aniline dyes to make pictures, create illusions, obscure or clarify structure or create a tension between painted and natural parts.[59]

Although the new studio furnituremakers are responding to a changed conception of design, the transformation from the Zen-like introspection of the 1950s woodworker to the McLuhanesque worldliness of the 1980s furnituremaker has not been accepted by all. Many first-generation woodworkers, who blazed the trail and inspired the following generation, criticize the new work. Maloof, a self-taught woodworker, feels that the domination of college training has divorced the craftsperson from the real world and resulted in work of great "preciousness."[60] George Nakashima, who emphasizes that design is dictated by material, finds the new emphasis on personal expression to be misguided. "Where you start with a concept and then you try to execute it in almost any material . . . it's the wrong use of wood." The emphasis on concept first, then technique and material, is to Nakashima "just simply crap."[61] Art Carpenter thoroughly articulated the reservations of the first generation in an exhibition review for *Fine Woodworking* in 1983. Distrusting the emphasis on play, pun, or farce, sensing that there was little concern for technique, and basing judgments primarily on conservative notions of utility, Carpenter labeled the new work as "artiture." To the author "most artiture pieces had little to do with wood and less to do with craftsmanship."[62]

Carpenter felt that ego and a concern for higher prices had driven this new work, but in fact most of the work he reviewed was well made, using wood as the primary material. What distinguished it was the attempt of the makers to use wood and traditional techniques in a different context. They sought to explore more varied and challenging avenues, to make the pieces "useful, fun, individual, and visually pleasing."[63] As Wendy Maruyama explains about her own background and teaching philosophy, "Although I feel an obligation to teach the traditions of woodworking, I also hold strong to the ideas of experimentation with concepts, rather than falling back on what's been done before."[64]

The subject of Carpenter's review—a series of exhibitions and gallery shows that featured work of the second generation—reflects the continued strength of the educational training system, the development of a national network, and the emergence of new opportunities. The number and type of schools that offered a woodworking education continued to increase in the 1980s. By 1985, about twenty colleges offered full-time degree programs in furniture, while furniture design and construction courses were available in approximately fifty other colleges or in a number of craft centers through the country.[65] Instructors from the degree programs invited other teachers or studio furnituremakers to participate in instruction, by slide lectures, workshops, or residence. Such interaction has broken down older regional barriers—for example, the rounded-edge California work or the crisp angular work of RIT of the 1970s—and fostered a national network that stimulates ideas, identifies needs, and provides a professional identity. The establishment of this national network and interest in professional identity led to the formation of the Society of Furniture Artists (SOFA) in 1985. The organization sought to address common issues for "designers and builders of objects in wood." Its first newsletter emphasized the importance of good analytical and critical writing and the need for furnituremakers to exchange ideas and concepts as well as technical information.[66]

The vitality of communication can be seen in the enormous success of *Fine Woodworking*, a magazine established in 1976 to appeal to amateur and studio furnituremakers. As it has flourished in the 1980s, *Fine Woodworking* has sponsored a series of design books (1977, 1979, 1983, and 1987), covered shows, featured biographies of studio furnituremakers, and served an important role in the dissemination of technical knowledge. The magazine and such ancillary activities as video tapes and books both drive and reflect the healthy state of contemporary furniture in general and studio work in particular.[67]

The increasing sophistication of the studio furniture market can be most easily seen in the emergence of new venues for show and sales. In the 1960s and 1970s, studio furnituremakers who wanted to show their work were restricted to small craft shops, ACC craft fairs (which emphasized sales to retailers), and small regional museums or craft centers. In the 1980s, increasing numbers of craft and art galleries, more professional national exhibitions, active participation of larger museums, and more direct sales have all contributed to and reflected the health of studio furniture. Bernice Wollman and Judy Coady at Workbench Gallery in New York developed theme shows that charted the development of the field. Beginning with a one-man show of Garry Knox Bennett's work in 1980, Workbench Gallery continued a program that included a show of works by PIA faculty and students, one of work by women only, and one in which the makers were required to work in several media. In 1981, Herta Loeser of the Society of Arts and Crafts in Boston began to show PIA furniture also. Other important galleries included Pritam & Eames, established in East Hampton, Long Island, in 1980 by Warren and Bebe Johnson, and Snyderman Gallery, established in Philadelphia in 1983 by Rick and Ruth Snyderman. These two galleries assembled stables of artists, mounted special exhibitions, and stimulated interest in commissions. Pritam & Eames and Snyderman continue to show the work of both established and new talent.[68]

The dramatic commercial turning point, however, occurred in 1983. Wendell Castle, whose *trompe l'oeil* work of the late 1970s had received critical acclaim but generated few sales, recognized the strength of the new second-generation work and its match with contemporary needs. With the encouragement of his New York gallery representative, Sandy Milliken, Castle devoted his considerable energies and resources from 1981 until 1983 to the production of historically based pieces made with exquisite woods and refined technique. In direct opposition to Modernism, Castle claimed "more is more." Although much of the work was well designed and aesthetically successful, its importance was more in its impact upon the marketplace. Milliken marketed the work aggressively, presenting "workmanship as art," and sold a desk and two chairs for $75,000, which far exceeded any previous price for studio furniture. Milliken's effective advertising and the prices of the work drew attention throughout both art and craft worlds.[69]

In direct response to the 1983 Milliken show and the increasing visibility of second-generation work, interest in studio furniture greatly expanded. The number of advertisements for furniture shows in *American Craft* increased noticeably in late 1983 and the announcements themselves became more polished. Galleries that had formerly shown only fine arts, such as Henoch in New York, and Clark and NAGA in the Boston area, began to show studio furniture consistently. Wider interest was not restricted to the East Coast: Hokin Kaufman Gallery in Chicago hosted an annual furniture show entitled "Furniture of the Eighties," beginning in 1983. Another annual Chicago event, "New Art Forms," began in 1986 and placed furniture within a mainstream context of twentieth-century decorative arts, including glass, ceramics, and fiber. "New Art Forms" and "American Craft at the Armory" presented mature second-generation work in a polished new environment.

As the number of studio-furniture galleries and of art galleries accepting the work grew, new markets emerged. Previously most work was simply purchased spontaneously or commissioned for specific use, but in the 1980s a few individuals such as Ronald and Anne Abramson, Virginia and Andrew Lewis, and Peter Joseph began to acquire broadly from numerous craftspeople. Museums have also demonstrated an interest in the world of second-generation work. Smaller museums like the Brockton Art Museum, Rhode Island School of Design Museum of Art, and Yale University Art Gallery, as well as larger institutions like the Oakland Museum, Detroit Institute of Arts, and Museum of Fine Arts, Boston, have acquired the work of the new generation.

Two important museum exhibitions followed,

"Material Evidence: New Color Techniques in Handmade Furniture," organized by the Renwick Gallery of the National Museum of American Art, Smithsonian Institution, and Workbench Gallery in 1984; and "Craft Today: Poetry of the Physical," a 1986 exhibition at the American Craft Museum. In 1984, Coady and Wollman of the Workbench Gallery invited nineteen leading second-generation studio furnituremakers to make and exhibit furniture made using ColorCore, a solid colored laminate. All of the participants had demonstrated an ability to retain some aspect of utility in their work while emphasizing social, emotional, and intellectual content. The resulting exhibition, which traveled to the Renwick Gallery in 1985, was well received by design and art critics who became enchanted with the structural integrity, rich ornament, and refined details of the work. To many, the work answered the shortcomings of the Memphis furniture and pointed out the vitality of an American design located in the studio rather than in industry.[70]

"Craft Today: Poetry of the Physical," an encyclopedic exhibition intended to document this vitality of American work in all media, also indicated the strength of the second generation's work. Illusion, emotion, irony, and ornament were explored in works made predominantly of wood, often painted or mixed with other materials, and displaying high levels of skilled workmanship. The orthodoxy of the 1950s had given way to a more pluralistic vision unified by its insistence on solid concept, appropriate materials and techniques, and good workmanship.[71]

By the late 1980s, the second-generation furnituremakers have established a firm middle ground between antique reproductions and first-generation reverence for natural wood and overtly functional works in safe styles, and the radical new art furniture of Robert Wilson, Scott Burton, and Howard Meister. Reflecting its makers' recognition of their heritage and particular strengths, the mature work fills a particular need for participatory visual art — sometimes sensual, sometimes functional, sometimes intimate, sometimes a combination. Each piece of furniture can evoke a variety of emotional responses. The makers have met the challenge of cultural utility by means of admirable workmanship, decorative treatments, and meaningful composition. They have recognized and embraced the distinguishing features of small-shop, high-end custom cabinetmakers: broad technical repertoire, ability and willingness to change designs quickly or even in process, flexibility that permits taking chances and exploring variation to create fresh statements that build upon and reinterpret the confluence of past and present, and clientele whose price range can accommodate such attention to composition and execution.[72]

By building upon these strengths and maintaining a strong dialectic between concept, material, and technique, the studio furnituremaker will continue to find a market. As with cabinetmakers of the past, some will achieve economic success, others will struggle; but their work will survive and document the vitality of functional artistic objects in America in the 1980s.

1. Recent critics who have commented upon this include Matthew Kangas and Joseph Giovannini: Matthew Kangas, "The Embodiment of Ingenuity," *American Craft* 47, no. 4 (August/September 1987), pp. 46–53; Joseph Giovannini, "Wendell Castle: Occupying the Blur," in Edward S. Cooke, Jr., Joseph Giovannini, and Davira Taragin, *Furniture by Wendell Castle* (Detroit: Founder's Society of the Detroit Institute of Arts; and New York: Hudson Hills; 1989).

2. On the demise of Modernism and the need for new art to counter the staleness of neo-Modernism, a useful collection of essays is Brian Wallis, ed., *Art After Modernism: Rethinking Representation* (New York: The New Museum of Contemporary Art, 1984).

3. Within this catalogue, I use the term *studio furniture* since I find it the clearest term. Other publications have used terms such as *handmade furniture*, *art furniture*, or even *artiture*, but each of these is misleading or highly subjective: *handmade* implies that the craftsperson eschews any machinery in a romantic Ruskinian way; *art furniture* is a term with a very historical meaning referring to small-shop custom work in the last quarter of the nineteenth century; and *artiture* was originally used in a derogatory manner. *Studio furniture* is a more objective term since it conveys: an education based in the colleges rather than apprenticeship; the importance of a vigorous conceptual approach to design and construction; and the small scale of operation distinguished from factories or manufactories.

4. On the period use of the term "first generation," see *Craft Horizons* 26, no. 3 (June 1966) and *American Crafts '76: An Aesthetic View* (Chicago: Museum of Contemporary Art, 1976).

5. Folklorist Henry Glassic explains *bricolage* in a craftsperson's conceptual stage in "Folk Art," Richard Dorson, ed., *Folklore and Folklife* (Chicago: University of Chicago Press, 1972), esp. pp. 259–60.

6. The earlier roots in the Aesthetic and Arts and Crafts Movements are best discussed in various recent publications: *In Pursuit of Beauty: Americans and the Aesthetic Movement* (New York: The Metropolitan Museum of Art and Rizzoli, 1987); and Wendy Kaplan, ed., *"The Art That is Life": The Arts & Crafts Movement in America, 1875–1920* (Boston: Museum of Fine Arts, Boston, 1987). The importance of the 20s and 30s has not been fully explored but suggestive studies include Eileen Boris, *Art and Labor: Ruskin, Morris, and the Craftsman Ideal in America* (Philadelphia: Temple University Press, 1986), esp. pp. 126–31 and 189–93; and David Whisnant, *All That is Native & Fine: The Politics of Culture in an American Region* (Chapel Hill: The University of North Carolina Press, 1983).

7. Nigel Whiteley, "Toward a Throw-Away Culture: Consumerism, 'Style Obsolescence' and Cultural Theory in the 1950s and 1960s," *The Oxford Art Journal* 10, no. 2 (1987), pp. 3–27.

8. See Sharon Darling, *Chicago Furniture: Art, Craft & Industry, 1833–1983* (New York: W.W. Norton, 1984), pp. 311–17.

9. Arthur Poulos, *The American Design Adventure, 1940–1975* (Cambridge, Mass.: MIT Press, 1988), pp. 78–103.

10. R. Craig Miller, "Interior Design and Furniture", in *Design in America: The Cranbook Vision, 1925–1950* (New York: Harry N. Abrams, 1983), pp. 108–43.

11. Poulos, pp. 79–83; and *Craft Horizons* 19, no. 2 (March/April), pp. 38–39.

12. Poulos, pp. 98–103.

13. Good biographies of Esherick and Nakashima are included in Michael Stone, *Contemporary American Woodworkers* (Salt Lake City: Peregrine Smith, 1986), pp. 2–33. See also *Woodenworks* (St. Paul: Minnesota Museum of Art, 1972); *The Wharton Esherick Museum: Studio and Collection* (Paoli, Penn.: The Wharton Esherick Museum, 1977); George Nakashima, *The Soul of a Tree* (New York: Kodanska International Ltd. 1981); John Kelsey, "George Nakashima," *Fine Woodworking* 14 (January/February 1979): 40–46; and Derek Ostergard, *George Nakashima: Full Circle* (New York: American Craft Museum, 1989).

14. *Woodenworks*, p. 22.

15. New York: Reinhold Publishing Co., 1956.

16. On Maloof and Carpenter, see Stone, pp. 64–99; Glenn Loney, "Sam Maloof," *Craft Horizons* 31, no. 4 (August 1971), pp. 16–19 and 70; Rick Mastelli, "Sam Maloof," *Fine Woodworking* 25 (November/December 1980), pp. 48–55; Sam Maloof, *Sam Maloof, Woodworker* (New York: Kodanska International Ltd., 1983); and Rick Mastelli, "Art Carpenter," *Fine Woodworking* 37 (November/December 1982), pp. 62–68. Weed, who was praised often in the 1950s, has not enjoyed the same visibility, but see Richard Starr, "Portfolio: Walker Weed," *Fine Woodworking* 38 (January/February 1983), pp. 66–69.

17. On the evolution of the School for American Craftsmen, see *Craft Horizons* 4, no. 8 (February 1945), p. 1; *Craft Horizons* 4, no. 10 (August 1945), pp. 4–9, and 35; *Craft Horizons* 5, no. 13 (May 1946), p. 5; *Craft Horizons* 8, no. 21 (May 1948): 14; and Harold Brennan, "The School for American Craftsmen," *Craft Horizons* 20, no. 36 (May/June 1960), pp. 21–24. Quotation is from *Interiors*, April 1946, as quoted by Poulos in *The American Design Adventure*, p. 170.

18. John Kelsey, "Tage Frid," *Fine Woodworking* 52 (May/June 1985), p. 71.

19. Esherick quotation is from *Craft Horizons* 26, no. 3 (June 1966), p. 18. Other period ideas about the role of machinery can be found in *Craft Horizons* 3, no. 7 (November 1944), p. 23; *Craft Horizons* 4, no. 8 (February 1945), pp. 16–17, and 36; and Norman Cherner, "Relating Design to Our Times," *Craft Horizons* 8, no. 22 (August 1948), pp. 19–21.

20. Greta Daniel's article "Furniture by Craftsmen" in *Craft Horizons* 17, no. 2 (March–April 1957), pp. 34–38, articulates clearly the emphasis on wood as the major aesthetic and design feature. See also *Craft Horizons* 6, no. 5 (November 1946), pp. 5–7.

21. Quotations taken from a 1966 conversation among Sam Maloof, Wharton Esherick, and Donald McKinley, as transcribed in *Craft Horizons* 26, no. 3 (June 1966), pp. 15–19.

22. *Craft Horizons* 6, no. 5 (November 1946), p.6.

23. A particularly good summary of these changes is Marcia Manhart and Tom Manhart, "The Widening Arcs: A Personal History of a Revolution in the Arts," in Marcia Manhart and Tom Manhart, eds., *The Eloquent Object: The Evolution of American Art in Craft Media Since 1945* (Tulsa, Okla.: The Philbrook Museum of Art, 1987), pp. 15–65. Another valuable source is a roundtable discussion held April 4 and 14, 1976, and transcribed in *Craft Horizons* 36, no. 3 (June 1976): 37–52.

24. Rose Slivka, "The American Craftsman/1964," *Craft Horizons* 24, no. 3 (May/June 1964), p. 32, but see also pp. 10–11, 33, 112–13, and 126.

25. Slivka's tireless call for crafts to follow fine arts in order to gain acceptance is best summarized in her autobiographical "The Art/Craft Connection: A Personal, Critical, and Historical Odyssey," *The Eloquent Object*, pp. 67–103. See also Slivka, "The Object: Function, Craft, and Art," *Craft Horizons* 25, no. 5 (September/October 1965), pp. 10–11; and Giovannini, "Wendell Castle: Occupying the Blur."

26. Slivka, "The American Craftsman/1964," p. 11; Slivka, "The New Ceramic Presence," *Craft Horizons* 21, no. 4 (July/August 1961): 30–37; Slivka, "The New Tapestry," *Craft Horizons* 23, no. 2 (March/April, 1963), pp. 10–19.

27. The letters to the editors in *Craft Horizons* from 1961 through much of the 1960s are filled with such reactions, but especially rich letters can be found in *Craft Horizons* 26, no. 2 (March/April 1966), p. 8; and *Craft Horizons* 26, no. 3 (June 1966), p. 6.

28. A good biographical study of Westermann is Barbara Haskell, *H.C. Westermann* (New York: Whitney Museum of American Art, 1978). His ideas about craftsmanship are quoted on pages 20 and 21.

29. Artschwager quoted by Jan McDevitt in "The Object: Still Life," *Craft Horizons* 25, no. 5 (September/October 1965), p. 54. See also McDevitt, pp. 28–30; and Richard Armstrong, *Artschwager, Richard* (New York: W.W. Norton, 1988).

30. "Fantasy Furniture" was the first furniture exhibition to attract wide coverage: *Craft Horizons* 26, no. 2 (March/April 1966), p. 4.

31. A recent analysis of Castle's career is Edward Cooke, Jr., and Davira Taragin, "The Career of Wendell Castle," in *Furniture by Wendell Castle*; but also see *Woodenworks*; and Stone, pp. 114–29.

32. *Touching Wood* (Portsmouth, Ohio: Southern Ohio Museum and Cultural Center, 1981), p. 8. For additional information on Simpson and examples of his early work, see "Fantasy Furniture," *Craft Horizons* 26, no. 1 (January/February 1966), pp. 14–15; Marshall Davidson, "Wooden Wiles of Tommy Simpson," *Craft Horizons* 38, no. 1 (February 1978), pp. 45–47, and 67; and *Perspectives: Tommy Simpson* (Sheboygan, Wisc.: John Michael Kohler Arts Center, 1982).

33. For example, *Craft Horizons*'s summary of the 1964 "American Craft Show" illustrated 129 pieces of ceramic, 52 of fiber, and only 7 of wood. Not only was wood scarce in exhibitions, but the designs were seen as derivative of colonial vernacular and modern styles with little attempt to be more adventurous: *Craft Horizons* 20, no. 5 (July/August 1960), p. 6; *Craft Horizons* 24, no. 3 (May/June 1964), pp. 92–93; *Craft Horizons* 26, no. 3 (June 1966), p. 75; and *Craft Horizons* 27, no. 3 (May/June 1967), p. 65.

34. The best sources for Osgood are Stone, pp. 144–59; and Rosanne Somerson, "Perfect Sweep," *American Craft* 45, no. 3 (June/July 1985), pp. 30–34. He wrote about his techniques in a number of articles: "Bent Laminations," *Fine Woodworking* 6 (spring 1977), pp. 35–38; "Tapered Lamination," *Fine Woodworking* 14 (January/February 1979), pp. 48–51; and "Bending Compound Curves," *Fine Woodworking* 17 (July/August 1979), pp. 57–60.

35. Jackson has received little attention until recently, but see David Hank's brief entry on him in *Philadelphia: Three Centuries of American Art* (Philadelphia: Philadelphia Museum of Art, 1976). The best documentation on Jackson's influence as both teacher and furniture-maker is Franklin Parrasch, *A Tribute to Daniel Jackson* (Washington, D.C.: Franklin Parrasch Gallery, 1989).

36. The catalogues produced for the exhibitions provide good documentation: *Woodenworks*, and Lee Nordness, *Objects: USA* (New York: The Viking Press, 1970).

37. For a graphic example of Castle's influence, see Dona Meilach, *Creating Modern Furniture* (New York: Crown, 1975). On Castle's dissatisfaction, see Cooke and Taragin.

38. Cooke and Taragin.

39. Krenov's best explication of his philosophy is his earliest book, *A Cabinetmaker's Notebook* (New York: Van Nostrand Company, 1976). See also Stone, pp. 100–29.

40. Michael Stone provides a general biography of Zucca in "Skill at Play: Edward Zucca," *American Craft* 41, no. 3 (June/July 1981), pp. 2–5.

41. For information on Mattia, see Joy Cattanach Smith, "Furniture: A Sculptural Medium," *Art New England* 7, no. 1 (December–January 1985–86), pp. 4–5.

42. On the establishment of PIA, see *Craft Horizons* 35, no. 2 (April 1975) p. 6; and *Boston University Newsletter: Program in Artisanry* (winter 1977). Important information on the program has been provided in interviews with Jere Osgood, Tim Philbrick, and Bruce Beeken. See also Akiki Busch, "By Design," *Metropolis* 4, no. 7 (March 1985), pp. 31–33, 37–38; and David Sanders, "Portrait of a Program: Woodworking and Furniture Design at Boston University's Program in Artisanry," *The Workshop* 3 (fall 1983), pp. 10–11.

43. John Kelsey, "Two New Schools," *Fine Woodworking* 10 (spring 1978), p. 42; and Cooke and Taragin.

44. Nina Stritzler, *Pioneer and Pioneering 20th Century Women Furniture Designers & Furniture Designer/Makers* (New York: Bernice Steinbaum Gallery, 1988); Kenneth Trapp, "To Beautify the Useful: Benn Pitman and the Women's Woodcarving Movement in Cincinnati in the Late Nineteenth Century," in Kenneth Ames, ed., *Victorian Furniture* (Philadelphia: Victorian Society in America, 1983), pp. 174–192; Laura Cekanowicz, "Portfolio: Woodworking Women," *Fine Woodworking* 17 (July/August 1979), pp. 54–56; "Women Are Woodworking," *American Craft* 43, no. 1 (February/March 1983), pp. 44–45; and Terrie Noll, "Finding Your Own Voice," *Woodwork* 1 (spring 1989), pp. 36–41.

45. For a discussion of economic difficulties confronting furniture-makers of various sorts, see Roger Holmes, "Survivors," *Fine Woodworking* 55 (November/December 1985), pp. 91–97.

46. John Kelsey, "Craftsman's Gallery," *Fine Woodworking* 1, no. 3 (summer 1976), p. 10.

47. Cooke and Taragin; Jonathan Fairbanks, "Introduction," in *Sam Maloof: Woodworker*, p. 17; and files in the Museum of Fine Arts, Boston, archives.

48. "Young Americans," *Fine Woodworking* 2, no. 2 (fall 1977), pp. 82 and 84.

49. "Working Wonders with Wood: American Furnituremakers Working in Hardwood," *American Crafts* 39, no. 3 (June/July 1979), pp. 10–15; and John Kelsey, "Editor's Notebook," *Fine Woodworking* 18 (September/October 1979), p. 89.

50. *Fine Woodworking* 24 (September/October 1980), p. 92 illustrates the cabinet with the headline "Decoration vs. Desecration." Spirited responses can be found in subsequent letters to the editor: *Fine Woodworking* 25 (November/December 1980), p. 4; and *Fine Woodworking* 26 (January/February 1981), p. 8. For more information on Bennett, see Stone, pp. 130–143.

51. On the reexamination in all fields, see Brian Wallis, ed., *Art after Modernism: Rethinking Representation* (New York: The New Museum of Contemporary Art, 1984).

52. Robert Venturi, *Complexity and Contradiction in Architecture* (New York: Museum of Modern Art, 1966); and Venturi, *Learning from Las Vegas* (Cambridge: MIT Press, 1972).

53. Margolin develops this distinction in "Consumers and Users: Two Publics for Design," in *Phoenix: New Attitudes in Design* (Toronto:

Queen's Quay terminal, 1984), pp. 48–55. The whole volume provides good insight into design since World War II.

54. The best summary of Memphis is Barbara Radice, *Memphis: Research, Experiences, Results, Failure and Successes of New Design* (New York: Rizzoli, 1984).

55. On the structure of the Italian furniture industry, see Josh Markel, "Furnituremaking in Italy: Competition and Cooperation," *Fine Woodworking* 58 (May/June 1986), pp. 50–53. On the relationship between 1950s Good Design and 1960s Pop, see Nigel Whiteley, "'Semi-Works of Art': Consumerism, Youth Culture and Chair Design in the 1960s," *Furniture History* 23 (1987), pp. 108–126.

56. Denise Domergue, *Artists Design Furniture* (New York: Harry N. Abrams, 1984); Barbara Jepson, "Art Furniture," *American Craft* 45, no. 5 (October/November 1985), pp. 10–17; and Robert Janjigian, *High Touch: The New Materialism in Design* (New York: E.P. Dutton, 1987).

57. Smith wrote this in a letter to the editor that responded to Art Carpenter's "Artiture": *Fine Woodworking* 40 (May/June 1983), p. 4. See also Lewis Buckner, "Ideas Go Further than Technique," *Fine Woodworking* 46 (May/June 1984), pp. 76–81.

58. *Fine Woodworking* 34 (May/June 1982), pp. 95–97; Dick Burrows, "Furniture from the Lathe," *Fine Woodworking* 59 (July/August 1986), pp. 34–40; and Graham Blackburn, "The Platejoiner," *Woodwork* 1 (spring 1984), pp. 74–77.

59. *High Touch*; John Marlowe, "California Crossover," *Fine Woodworking* 61 (November/December 1986), pp. 60–64; Roger Holmes, "Color and Wood," *Fine Woodworking* 41 (July/August 1983), pp. 70–73.

60. Mastelli, "Sam Maloof," p. 54.

61. Kelsey, "George Nakashima," p. 46.

62. Arthur Espenet Carpenter, "The Rise of Artiture," *Fine Woodworking* 38 (January/February 1983), pp. 98–103.

63. Letter to the editor from studio furnituremaker Jim Fawcett, *Fine Woodworking* 40 (May/June 1983), p. 4.

64. Terrie Noll, "Finding Your Own Voice," *Woodwork* 1 (spring 1989), p. 39.

65. Larry Hunter, "Eleven Graduate Schools," *Fine Woodworking* 26 (January/February 1981), p. 36; and "Woodworking Week at Anderson Ranch," *Fine Woodworking* 55 (November/December 1985), p. 122.

66. *Society of Furniture Artists Newsletter* 1 (spring 1986), esp. pp. 1–3.

67. Paul Bertorelli, "A Tale of *Fine Woodworking*," *Craft International* 5, no. 2 (October/November/December 1985), p. 16; and Bertorelli, "Introduction," *Fine Woodworking Design Book Four* (Newtown, Conn.: The Taunton Press, 1987).

68. Leslie Cochran, "To Market, To Market: The Growing Interest in Handmade Furniture," *Craft International* 5, no. 2 (October/November/December 1985), pp. 13–15; Rick Mastelli, "New Furniture," *Fine Woodworking* 31 (November/December 1981), pp. 95–97; and Sarah Bodine, "Beyond the Final Polish: The Marketing of Handmade Furniture," *The Workshop* 3 (fall 1983), pp. 1–2.

69. See Cooke and Taragin.

70. *Material Evidence: New Color Techniques in Handmade Furniture* (Washington, D.C.: Smithsonian Institution, 1985). For a review of the exhibition, see Elizabeth Goldman, "Material Evidence," *The Workshop* 4 (spring 1984), pp. 1–3.

71. Paul Smith and Edward Lucie-Smith, *Craft Today: Poetry of the Physical* (New York: American Craft Museum, 1986).

72. Several recent articles have emphasized the importance of studio crafts people working on their own technical, functional, and effective strengths rather than following or rivaling other fields: Rob Barnard, "Craft in a Muddle," *New Art Examiner* 14, no. 6 (February 1987), pp. 24–27; Jane Addams Allen, "Comment," *American Craft* 48, no. 2 (April/May 1988), pp. 20 and 64; and Wayne Higby, "Comment," *American Craft* 49, no. 1 (February/March 1989), pp. 16–17. On the importance of a continuum with small-shop furnituremakers of the past, see Edward S. Cooke, Jr., "The Study of American Furniture from the Perspective of the Maker," in Gerald W.R. Ward, ed., *Perspectives on the Study of American Furniture* (New York: W.W. Norton, 1988).

BRUCE BEEKEN AND JEFF PARSONS

1 CHILD'S BED
Shelburne, Vermont, 1989
Maple; sycamore veneer; chromed brass, silk cord,
canvas, futon
H: 27¾ in., W: 35¾ in., L: 67 in.
Loaned by Bruce Beeken and Jeff Parsons

Bruce Beeken (b. 1953) and Jeff Parsons (b. 1956) comprise a
partnership that brings together the technical sophistication
and efficiency of a production shop and the expressive qualities of one-of-a-kind studio work. Seeking the flexibility to
undertake production jobs, exhibition work, or, ideally, a
combination of both, they have achieved a rare balance of
"productivity, personal involvement, and experimentation that
integrates technical and aesthetic concerns in an economically
viable fashion."[1] The constant interplay between stripped-
down form and such production methods as shaping and
bending results in subtle and deceptively simple designs.

Beeken is the impulsive, more lyrical half of the partnership. Growing up in New Hampshire, he developed an affinity
for the woodland. While hiking and canoeing he acquired a
special respect for Native American lore and its ideal of a spiritual coexistence with nature. The lure of living in the woods
and working wood led him to apprentice with Carl Bausch, a
canoemaker in Charlotte, Vermont, who combined traditional
lines with innovative techniques. While building lightweight,
durable, and well-crafted boats, Beeken became more and
more keen about methods of working wood and excited by
making things. Within a year of beginning his apprenticeship,
however, he began to believe that furnituremaking would offer
greater creative potential.

Beeken apprenticed in 1974 with Simon Watts, a cabinetmaker in Putney, Vermont, who makes very straightforward
furniture in the manner of first-generation studio woodworkers.[2] Watts trained Beeken to cut dovetails and other traditional joints, to turn on a lathe, and to bend wood. At the same
time, Beeken learned about studio furniture from his school
friend Kirk Powlowski, who attended the Rochester Institute
of Technology and introduced Beeken to the work of Wendell
Castle, James Krenov, and others. Beeken enrolled in Boston
University's Program in Artisanry (PIA), attracted by its faculty—intially Krenov and then Jere Osgood—and by the
program's integration of design and bench work. PIA had a

Fig. a. Trundle bed. New England, 1700–50. Oak, pine. H: 19½ in.,
W: 47½ in., L: 62 in. Museum of Fine Arts, Boston. Gift of a Friend of the
Department of American Decorative Arts and Sculpture 1977.801.

Fig. b.   Side chair. Boston, Massachusetts, 1976. Maple; leather. H: 31 in., W: 17 in., D: 16½ in. Private collection.

profound effect upon him—Dan Jackson prodded him to shun an easy traditional approach; Jere Osgood provided a role model for the sensitive use of wood; Alphonse Mattia showed him how beautifully furniture could be made; and such fellow students as James Schriber and Tim Philbrick provided important stimulation. His student work (fig. b) suggests a very mature hand that had mastered the liberating lessons of Jackson and Osgood.

Upon graduation in 1978, Beeken returned to Vermont, setting up shop in Burlington and focusing upon exhibition and commission work. At first he continued making graceful, lyrical work that made little use of machines, relying instead on direct handshaping. "I prefer simple work that is made in wooden ways. Time and familiarity add to the character of the things that we live around and their use makes us fond of them."[3] In late 1980 he moved his shop to an enormous barn on the Shelburne Farm estate of the Webb family and met

some of the younger architects in the Burlington area. His work in 1981 and 1982 embodies a new approach to design: the forms were massed like buildings, the individual elements were large, and construction was exposed. In preparation for the 1982 show "Color/Wood," organized by his friend Schriber at the Brookfield Craft Center, Beeken decorated a great chest with block-printed red apples and green leaves.[4] In subsequent work he tried gold-leafed and silk-screened images, the forms of which were simplified and readily adaptable to limited production runs. In 1983, Depot Woodworking, a Burlington production woodshop specializing in architectural work, commissioned Beeken to design a piece for a new line of furniture. He accepted on the condition that Jeff Parsons, then working at Depot, would build the prototype piece in Beeken's shop. Beeken had known Parsons from PIA, respected his work, and realized that he was "bilingual"—conversant with philosophies, demands, and techniques of both custom shops and production shops.

Parsons had also graduated from PIA, earning a B.A.A. in 1979, but his experiences had been very different from Beeken's. Before entering PIA, Parsons had worked for a manufacturer of banjo and girandole clocks. PIA, therefore, not only introduced him to the wide possibilities of design and new technical advances, but also provided the solid cabinetmaking foundation he lacked. The varied uses of wood and other materials, the wide assortment of techniques, and the wide-ranging approach to design fascinated him. He was particularly impressed by the clarity of design, respect for materials, and direct approach of Osgood, Peder Moos, and Hans Wegner. Parson's interest in the Scandinavian ideal of craftspeople working in production shops led him to work for a frame-making manufactory in New Hampshire for two years before going to work for Depot in 1981.

In working on the prototype in 1983, Beeken and Parsons found that they complemented each other very well. They shared similar assumptions, vocabulary, and knowledge about furniture, but each contributed a special strength to a partnership. While Beeken had an intuitive sense of design, proportions, and detail, Parsons had developed an ability to derive form from methods of construction. After working on the prototype, they formed a real partnership. Their initial jobs ranged from designing a kitchen to redesigning the Adirondack chair. For the latter, they used tapering and pattern shaping techniques to make a solid wood, functional outdoor chair that would sit better and last much longer than the original "carpenter-cobbed" examples.[5] In the early years of the partnership, they also did a great deal of subcontracted work: they developed prototypes, made a run of chairs designed by Wendell Castle for Arc International, and developed jigs for production pieces. These jobs permitted Beeken and Parsons to add needed equipment and refine their teamwork. They have become recognized for their talents in three-dimensional pattern shaping, most recently making an edition of bent-laminated Brushstroke chairs and foot stools designed by Roy Lichtenstein. These projects for other shops, artists, and design professionals helped Beeken and Parsons develop an ability to conceptualize ideas individually, discuss and collaborate to resolve and clarify ideas, and thereby stretch themselves conceptually and technically. Easily and precisely made with shaper jigs and other machinery, their tightly resolved

Fig. c.   Side chair. Shelburne, Vermont, 1987. Elm; wet formed leather. H: 30 in., W: 19 in., D 19 in. Private collection.

forms interweave "heart and soul" as expressions of personal experience, their relationship to the region, technical efficiency, and integrated decoration (fig. c).

A child's bed (cat. 1) clearly integrates personal ideas and the technical and artistic lessons of the contracted work.[6] As recent fathers, Beeken and Parsons were drawn to a seventeenth-century trundle bed (fig. a); they updated the form by designing a bed that features a futon supported by canvas laced into the frame. The curved head- and footboards that float between upright legs are based on the form of a bed that Beeken had made in 1981. Using a shaper and some hand-shaping, they made tapered straight legs, then used a jigged router to dish and taper the headboard and footboard. To glue and taper the sycamore veneer over the maple core, they reused the template that had established the router jig. Functional decorative elements make reference to the insides: the chromed brass discs secure the silk eyelets through which the canvas is laced, and echo the grommets of the canvas; the silk cord of the eyelets resembles the lacing for the canvas; and its color picks up the red quilting stitches of the futon.

1.   Quotation from response to author's questionnaire; other biographical information from Beeken's and Parsons's resumes, and conversations with author, especially May and June 1989.

2.   For more on Watts, see *Woodforms* (Brockton, Mass.: Brockton Museum of Art, 1981).

3.   *Recent Art Furniture* (Niagara Falls, N.Y.: Niagara University, 1982), p. 9. A good example of his work from this period is his tea cart based on nineteenth-century tools and vehicles: *Bentwood Furniture* (Providence: Museum of Art, Rhode Island School of Design, 1984), pp. 20–21.

4.   See Roger Holmes, "Color and Wood," *Fine Woodworking* 41 (July/August 1983), p. 73.

5.   Bruce Beeken and Jeff Parsons, "Adirondack Chair," *Fine Woodworking* 52 (May/June 1985), pp. 46–49. The article provides a good discussion of the partnership's philosophies, techniques, and goals.

6.   Discussion of the bed is based on conversations with the author and a letter from Beeken to the author, January 21, 1989.

GARRY KNOX BENNETT

2 *BOSTON KNEEHOLE*
Oakland, California, 1989
Honduran rosewood, maple; aluminum, brick, Fountainhead, ColorCore, antiqued bronze; watercolor paint
H: 31¼ in., W: 50¼ in., D: 24 in.
Loaned by Garry Knox Bennett

Garry Knox Bennett (b. 1934) has played an important role in freeing studio furniture from an unbending reverence for wood and an obsession with technique. Although Bennett strives to be irreverent in both design and execution, loudly proclaiming a distaste for time-consuming workmanship and a fondness for expedience, he has, ironically, become a consummate designer and technician. The natural ease of his final product actually obscures the well-developed intuitive sense and wide-ranging skills of its maker. His direct and spontaneous work of the 1980s—characterized by exaggerated shapes made of mixed media and with carefully balanced details—has established him as one of the most successful furnituremakers.

Bennett developed his visual skills as a fine arts major at the California College of Arts and Crafts from 1958 until 1962.[1] Especially attracted by the sculpture of Noguchi and Brancusi, Bennett embarked on a career as a metal sculptor. Although he built a house and did some cabinetry work just after college, he preferred the malleability of metal. In 1963 Bennett drew on his metalworking skills and sculptural sense to tap a burgeoning market in California—hand-crafted roach clips and jewelry decorated with peace symbols. His success led, in 1966, to the establishment of Squirkenworks, a large metal plating and jewelry business. Financially secure, Bennett turned to his interest in sculptural metalworking.

In the early 1970s Bennett focused upon clocks, making cartoonlike forms with organic petallike curves or wings. Constructed of brass and aluminum with plated and painted details (fig. b), these clocks were sold at Gump's Gallery in San Francisco as well as galleries in New York, Illinois, and Arizona. Bennett found the genre's size and basic functional parameters ideal: he was able to work directly with the metal, and to make a clock in a day or two. During the 1970s Bennett gradually broadened his repertoire to include lamps and small chests of drawers. As he gained confidence in his building of functional art, he began to think of larger forms and different materials such as wood: "Wood is not as forgiving as metal,

Fig. a.   Kneehole bureau table. New York, about 1760. Mahogany, yellow poplar. H: 33⅛ in., W: 32⅛ in., D: 19¾ in. Museum of Fine Arts, Boston. The M. and M. Karolik Collection of 18th Century American Art 1939.127

Fig. b.   Clock. Oakland, California, 1975. Brass, gold plate, silver plate, ivory. H: 8 in., W: 12 in., D: 3 in. Private collection.

Fig. c.   Bench. Oakland, California, 1983. Yellow poplar, Honduran mahogany, walnut; paint. H: 22 in., W: 60 in., D: 20 in. Private collection.

but it's a rapid medium for making fairly large objects."[2] Using simple rabetted and nailed joinery, Bennett constructed wooden bases for his clocks and lamps and thus entered the world of furnituremaking.

Influenced by the growing interest in studio furniture, Bennett grew more concerned with technique, and experimented with more time-consuming joinery. Once he had mastered some woodworking skills, however, he quickly demonstrated his particular perspective. For a 1979 show at the Elaine Potter Gallery, he made a padouk cabinet that featured his most technically sophisticated work to date: dovetailed carcass, miter joints, bent laminated glazed doors, and secret latches. But, to announce his unwillingness to accept the means as an end unto itself, he drove a 16p nail into the smooth surface. The bent nail and and its surrounding hammer-head impressions signalled Bennett's reaction against the technical preciousness of much fine woodworking: "I wanted to make a statement that I thought people were getting a little too goddamn precious with their technique. I think tricky joinery is just to show, in most instances, you can do tricky joinery."[3] Bennett retained his eagerness to make functional furniture, but wanted to employ efficient techniques to explore bold new forms.

Having established his reputation as a free spirit, Bennett went on to explore the look or construction of furniture in several different blocks. In 1981 and 1982, he produced a series of wooden benches with similar composition: a thick wooden slab on four substantial straight legs, with solid band-sawn bolsters at each end. He explored texture in one bench, positive and negative space in another (fig. c), juxtaposition of Baltic birch plywood and gold leaf in another, and color in another. Painted decoration highlighted sections of some of these works.

Following the success of these benches, Bennett produced a series of trestle tables and desks from 1983 through 1985. At this point, Bennett again began to work with metal, combining wood, aluminum, brass, glass, and such synthetics as Formica. Large scale and a variety of media became Bennett's "signature." A 1985 trestle desk with band-sawn supports; wedged, through-tenoned painted tie beam; and decorative battens for the top was featured in the 1986 "Craft Today: Poetry of the Physical" exhibition at the American Craft Museum.[4]

The "Material Evidence: New Techniques in Handmade

Furniture" exhibition of 1984, organized by Workbench Gallery and the Renwick Gallery to encourage studio furniture-makers to explore the many possible uses of the synthetic material ColorCore, featured a desk derived from his trestle table series and a small side table. Bennett's work gained recognition as the most successful in that thematic show, and his desk (fig. d) set him on his current course of mixing Formica or ColorCore, aluminum, and some wood.

Series perfectly suit Bennett's methods of working. He eschews drawings, working directly with the material to realize his form. As he explains, "I have an isometric mind so I don't do any drawing except right on the wood, at the bandsaw. I figure out the next table while I'm making the current one. In my mind, each one fades into the next."[5] Like Hank Gilpin, Bennett relies on an intuitive compositional sense and well-honed technical repertoire. But while Gilpin favors wood, Bennett takes a broader approach, one based more on the possibilities of working metal and wood with such large machinery as bandsaws, drill presses, and milling machines. Most recently he has developed a series of small tables with cast legs and tops of Fountainhead, a *faux* granite used for kitchen counters. Bennett varies his work by changing the patina of the legs and the color of the tops.

Bennett's *Boston Kneehole* (cat. 2) typifies the graceful loudness of his furniture. Inspired by the classic elegance of a colonial form (fig. a), he produced a casually elegant form appropriate for contemporary use. The aluminum carcass, salmon ColorCore sides and salmon-and-orange ColorCore cockbead molding around the drawers, Fountainhead top, and salmon brick base all provide color and material counterpoints to the rosewood drawers to bestow a playful grace to the form. Bennett's ribboned profile also deviates from the bowed blocking of the original piece; it relies on bandsawn curves for its vitality. Other light touches include paint on the drawer bottoms and fronts of the kneehole doors and a locked safe behind these drawers. While the use of aluminum, ColorCore, and brick is unconventional in so classic a design, the precisely crafted joints, veneer, and molding make clear that the piece was conceived and executed as furniture.

Fig. d.   ColorCore Desk. Oakland, California, 1984. Rosewood; aluminum, ColorCore, gold-plated brass. H: 30½ in., W: 90 in., D: 30 in. Private collection.

1. Biographical information from Bennett's responses to author's questionnaire, May 1989; his resume; John Kelsey, "Portfolio: Garry Knox Bennett," *Fine Woodworking* 45 (March/April 1984), p. 79–81; Michael Stone, "Garry Knox Bennett," *American Craft* 44, no. 5 (October/November 1984), pp. 22–26; and Stone, *Contemporary American Woodworkers* (Salt Lake City: Peregrine Smith, 1986), pp. 130–143.

2. Stone, *Contemporary American Woodworkers*, p. 137.

3. *Ibid.*, p. 140.

4. *Material Evidence: New Color Techniques in Handmade Furniture* (Washington, D.C.: Smithsonian Institution, 1985), pp. 4–5 and 31; and Paul Smith and Edward Lucie-Smith, *Craft Today: Poetry of the Physical* (New York: American Craft Museum, 1986), pp. 154–155.

5. Kelsey, p. 79.

JOHN CEDERQUIST

3 *LE FLEURON MANQUANT*
Capistrano Beach, California, 1989
Baltic birch plywood; mahogany, Sitka spruce, purpleheart,
koa veneers; pigmented epoxy, aniline dye
H: 78⅝ in., W: 35 in., D: 12½ in.
Loaned by John Cederquist

John Cederquist (b. 1946) uses fixed-point perspective to
explore the relationship between reality and illusion. Alter-
nately disorienting and delighting, confusing and surprising,
his work challenges the viewer both visually and intellectually.

A graduate of California State University at Long Beach,
with a B.A. in art and an M.F.A. in crafts, Cederquist initially
followed the lead of Wendell Castle in the early 1970s.[1] Like
many others at that time, he was drawn to the anthropomorphic, organic qualities of Castle's shaping and began to make
similar sorts of sculpted containers, using molded leather
tubes and rings as textural counterpoints to the smoothly mod-
eled wood (fig. b). He also used steam bending and bent lamination to make Art Nouveau-based rockers and chairs. Both
his leather and bent work brought him national recognition.[2]

By 1981, having taught two- and three-dimensional design
at Saddleback College in Mission Viejo, California, since 1976,
Cederquist had grown dissatisfied with his existing body of
work and the tendency of many woodworkers to seek original
shapes in furniture. While executing perspective drawings of
his earlier work in three-quarter view and in profile, Cederquist became frustrated by the lack of correlation between the
real piece of furniture and the drawings. He turned to perspective drawing itself to establish direct and familiar contact
with the viewer. In 1981 he began to explore the possibilities
of pictorial rendering through perspective drawing, veneering
and inlaying, and photo-realist painting.[3]

The visual and technical roots of Cederquist's exploration
of pictorial image are several. From Japanese *Ukiyo-e* wood-
block prints, he borrowed the reliance on lines of varying qualities to provide definition between surface areas and deep
space, resulting in a contextual realism. From cartoon images
of the 1940s and 1950s, he studied the effects of black, white,
and gray compositions and learned the importance of camera
angles in exaggerating perspective. Cederquist began with a
notion of a fixed point of view for furniture, then sought to
depict it realistically in two dimensions by using wood grain

Fig. a.   High chest. John Townsend (1732–1809). Newport, Rhode Island,
about 1760. Mahogany, white pine. H: 87¼ in., W: 39 in., D: 20⅜ in.
Museum of Fine Arts, Boston. M. and M. Karolik Collection of 18th
Century American Arts 41.577.

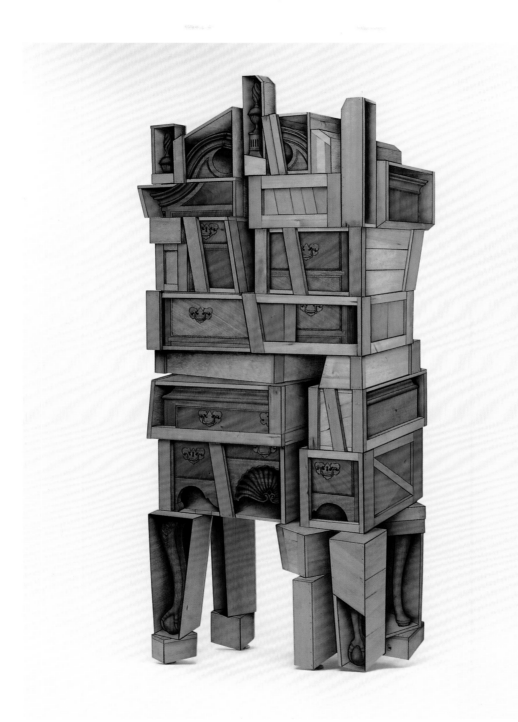

Fig. b. Wall cabinet. Costa Mesa, California, 1972. East Indian rosewood, padouk; collar leather. H: 37 in., W: 12 in., D: 8 in. Collection of John Cederquist.

and stain. Changes in wood grain indicate changes in plane or provide *trompe l'oeil* features; inlaid lines provide volume as well as *trompe l'oeil* effects.

In making a perspective piece, Cederquist begins by drawing directly on the Baltic birch plywood that he uses for the carcass. He then glues veneer with different grains over this drawing, using the lines and grain of the veneers to emphasize the drafted qualities of his work. Wood grain and inlaid lines are used to foreshorten planes and create the illusion of relief or hardware. This direct facade work precludes time-consuming preliminary sketches on paper and allows Cederquist to avoid complicated construction techniques. For most of his joints, he relies on router joinery. Even on case furniture with drawers, he builds simple mitered carcasses with parallelogram drawers.

Cederquist's initial experiments with furniture from a fixed-point perspective focused upon such relatively uncomplicated rectilinear forms as drafting tables or tables with

cross stretchers. These first pieces were not based upon specific prototypes but rather were composite images. By 1982, he had grown more confident in his new direction and began to work off of specific archetypal pieces of furniture—a chair from a Popeye cartoon; dressers, chairs, and game tables from the 1904 Thonet Bentwood catalogue (fig. c). In 1983, he also began to use notions of styles—Queen Anne or Art Deco—as a point of departure.

Cederquist's use of style language as picture and his interest in the ambiguous relationships between image and reality link him to the work of surrealists in the 1920s and 1930s, especially René Magritte. Cederquist uses rendering conventions and proportional distortions to present a single correct view of his forms, and an unlimited number of other, not necessarily incorrect views. The viewer can thus search for the stable view that matches his sense of reality or be surprised by the distortions and abstractions. But Cederquist questions Magritte's basic premise that being and representing are not the same, that the object does not perform the same function as its image. Rather than relying on words and titles to make this separation, Cederquist relies on furniture images and function to add an additional level of ambiguity to his work. In this manner Cederquist is really exploring a new surrealist path in three dimensions.

Recently Cederquist has achieved yet another level of sophistication in his perspective work, a move away from verisimilitude without sacrificing the ambiguities of prototype object, illusion, and function.[4] He has begun to use less straightforward furniture forms and a broken plane front facade, rather than a simple flat facade, to reinforce the three-quarter perspective view. His first work in this fashion was a drawered cabinet that appeared to be a construction of stacked closed shipping crates.

At the same time that he made the stacked crates, Cederquist made *Le Fleuron Manquant* ("The Missing Finial"), a high chest that possesses a strong historical and illusionistic mix (cat. 3). He began with a high chest by John Townsend of Newport (fig. a), one of colonial America's master craftsmen. Cederquist sectioned the piece, borrowing a drafting technique seen in Thomas Chippendale's *Cabinetmaker's Director* of 1753, in which furniture forms are composite images depicting the various options for feet, legs, carving, and cornices. Cederquist then framed these sections as if individually crated, drawing inspiration from the story of another Newport piece of furniture at the Museum of Fine Arts, a desk-and-bookcase that had lost its central finial when it was returned from a loan exhibition. With the crate chest sparking his imagination, Cederquist envisioned a Newport piece in which the finials and other sections were packed in small open crates and stacked to create the whole.

In his high chest, Cederquist has faithfully represented the Townsend original by means of mahogany grain and inlaid and painted lines, then crated it with Sitka spruce veneer, shadowing, and foreshortened planes to reinforce the three-

quarter perspective. Parallelogram drawers slide on an angle that follows the point of view. Yet the drawers do not match the illusionary ones exactly, and some are operated with hinged finger openings. The drawers and their placement, combined with the deliberate fragmentation of the illusion, create a multi-layered reality that continually engages the eye and mind of the viewer.

1. Biographical information from an interview with the author, December 1986; and from Sharon Emanuelli, *John Cederquist: Deceptions* (Los Angeles: Craft & Folk Art Museum, 1983).
2. Cederquist had work in the 1979 "New Handmade Furniture" and 1980 "California Woodworking": *American Craft* 39, no. 3 (June/July 1979), p. 11; *California Woodworking* (Oakland: Oakland Museum, 1981), p. 9.
3. Emanuelli 1983 includes a very thorough discussion of Cederquist's early perspective work.
4. The inspiration for the high chest and its difference from his earlier work and from Magritte's work is explained in a letter to the author, April 1989. Cederquist has only recently looked closely at Magritte and finds there are unconscious parallels, not conscious emulation.

Fig. c.   *The Game Table.* Capistrano Beach, California, 1982. Maple, birch plywood; purpleheart inlay; dye. H: 48 in., W: 32 in., D: 21 in. Private collection.

PETER DEAN

4 CANYON TABLE
Charlestown, Massachusetts, 1989
Ash; curly ash veneer; acrylic paint
H: 30 in., W: 27⅝ in., L: 108 in.
Loaned by Peter Dean

Peter Dean (b. 1951) has played a very important role in emphasizing the designed aspects of studio furniture. Educated originally as an architect, he has combined his visual and spatial language skills with woodworking skills to produce influential work in the last five years.

Dean enjoyed shop classes as a youngster and, after graduation from high school, made models for The Architects Collaborative and for Jung/Brannen Associates.[1] Dean's strength in structural visualization led him to the Rhode Island School of Design (RISD). He majored in architecture, sharpening his visual awareness and acquiring an important foundation in the development of three-dimensional ideas. He was, however, turned off by "an intellectual pretentiousness that left me unmoved and unchanged"; he found the emphasis on rhetoric over form and the general effetism fostered arbitrary design standards and work that was neither aesthetically nor architecturally interesting.[2] Partially in response to this dissatisfaction, he took a woodworking course with Tage Frid. With a developing design sense and an existing knowledge of basic joinery, Dean produced furniture in a Danish modern style and quickly gained Frid's respect. Dean found furnituremaking a very enjoyable, pragmatic supplement to his architectural studies: Frid was unpretentious and provided straight answers, students were encouraged to contribute to a cumulative advancement rather than to reinvent the wheel, and Dean found satisfaction in building things that worked aesthetically, functionally, and compositionally.

Although Dean received a few commissions after his graduation in 1977, he did not immediately pursue furnituremaking as a career. After his first full year at RISD, he had suffered a spiritual-psychological crisis. In spite of academic success and professional potential, his life "lurched to a halt in a crisis of meaning." The ideas and friendship of theologian-analyst Morton Kelsey provided spiritual succor, and, after graduating from RISD, Dean did graduate work in theology and psychology at University of Notre Dame, where Kelsey taught. A course on mysticism, taught by John Dunne, C.S.C., intro-

Fig. a.   Trestle table. Attributed to Benjamin Clark (1644–1724). Medfield, Massachusetts, 1690–1720. Silver maple, white pine. H: 26³⁄₁₆ in., W: 24¾ in., L: 108½ in. Museum of Fine Arts, Boston. Helen and Alice Coburn Fund and Frederick Brown Fund 1980.446.

duced Dean to the short stories of William Morris. Inspired by Morris's linkage of social, personal, and aesthetic reform, Dean began to see furnituremaking as "a way of life and living."[3] At the same time Dean studied sculpture with Tuck Langland, making figurative sculpture and casting bronzes.

By the spring of 1981, Dean concluded his theological and psychological studies and returned East to pursue furniture-making. His sister Ann Dean Hathaway, a potter, suggested that he look into the Program in Artisanry (PIA) at Boston University for advanced study in design and woodworking. The teachers, students, and work impressed Dean, who began his Master's degree at PIA in September of 1981. The creative environment and technical variety fostered by Jere Osgood and Alphonse Mattia suited Dean perfectly. His first piece, a ladies' writing desk (fig. b), successfully combined his interests in architecture, theology, and craft. Its Romanesque barrel vault evokes the basic spiritualism of early Christian cathedrals; the repetition of a pavillion with a grid trellis under the desk and on one side suggests the unification of inner and outer spaces, symbolizing the union of inner and outer personalities; the pink-and-white checkered parquet writing surface recalls the marble entrance foyers of Venetian villas, offering an invitation to enter and experience the desk. The checkered pattern blurs the oppositional tensions of the two colors to create a calming and meditative effect. In an effort to increase his technical skills to match his design vocabulary and spiritual depth, Dean tended to use very self-conscious and labor intensive methods. Whether drawing on an Eastern, Egyptian, or early Christian vocabulary, his work of the mid-1980s can be characterized as beautiful and powerful, but esoteric, work.[4]

Within the past year, Dean transcended the preciousness of his cathartic work without losing the intellectual content. He has consciously sought to work in a more direct and immediate manner, maintaining high levels of compositional structure and spiritual content but seeking to more freely use his extensive technical skills. One of his first mature efforts was *Mitten Chest* of late 1988 (fig. c). Vaguely reminiscent of the forms and details of such British Arts and Crafts designers as M.H. Bailee-Scott and C.F.A. Voysey, the design is more serene than many earlier Dean pieces. The workmanship is of the highest standard yet does not dominate. The imagery, however, is rich both personally and historically. The four inset *stupa*-like panels are drawn from a dream of Dean's from the

Fig. b. Ladies' writing desk. Boston, Massachusetts, 1983. Bloodwood, pearwood, holly, maple; glass. H: 36½ in., W: 46½ in., D: 23½ in. Private collection.

mid-1970s in which he envisioned a long chest with four buddhalike statues.

Dean's *Canyon Table* of 1989 (cat. 4) manifests his continued development of freer, yet more personal work.[5] Inspired by the proportions, simple spirituality, and workmanlike manner of a seventeenth-century trestle table (fig. a), he envisioned the hundreds of conscious and unconscious decisions that imbued the original table with its beauty. To make a table in a twentieth-century vernacular style, Dean developed a direct form with little ornamentation. Looking for a native hardwood to evoke singleness of purpose and honesty, he found ash in the necessary dimensions and began to build the trestle substructure. He updated the tie beam by using bent lamination, but retained the aesthetics of pinned mortise-and-tenon joints. On this base Dean set a top of ash floorboards with curly ash veneer, bookmatched with a natural edge along the inside. The rough channel between the boards resembles a canyon, and implies that an inner energy—the tie beam—is breaking through to the outer world. This canyon imagery is reinforced by the striated tones of brushed base paint—depicting the stratigraphy of the earth along the walls of a canyon—and also softened slightly by the sponged overpaint. Disarmingly simple and beautiful, Dean's *Canyon Table* possesses a very subtle depth that demands quiet contemplation.

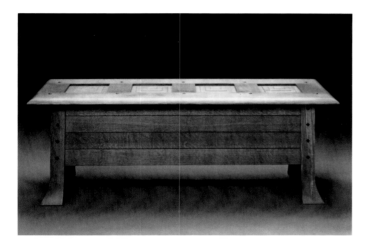

Fig. c. *Mitten Chest*. Charlestown, Massachusetts, 1988. White oak, ash, cedar; oil pigments. H: 18 in., W: 50 in., D: 17 in. Private collection.

1. Most biographical information from Dean's response to the author's questionnaire, May 1989; his resume; and conversations with the author, especially June 1989.
2. Questionnaire.
3. Conversation with the author, June 1989.
4. For example, Dean's *Ceremonial Side Table* of 1984 possessed a very strong Japanese feeling and featured a houselike structure with clapboards and windows under a glass top, suggesting the mutuality of inner and outer environments: *Material Evidence: New Color Techniques in Handmade Furniture* (Washington, D.C.: Smithsonian Institution, 1985), pp. 24–25.
5. Discussion of the table is based on conversation with the author, June 1989.

JOHN DUNNIGAN

5 TABLE
West Kingston, Rhode Island, 1989
Fiddleback mahogany; Rhodoid, silk crepe, silk cord and
tassels, upholstery buttons
Upholstered by Aarne Read
H: 30 in., W: 35 in., D: 17½ in.
Loaned by John Dunnigan

The furniture of John Dunnigan (b. 1950), documents the
change in the cultural environment between the first and
second generations of studio furnituremakers. Originally a
self-taught woodworker in search of a Bohemian lifestyle,
Dunnigan became a serious student of furniture design and
history, with an interest in classical civilization. His significant
body of work draws in fresh and innovative ways upon these
traditional foundations.

Although, as a teenager, Dunnigan worked at construction and carpentry jobs during the summers, he aspired to be

Fig. a.   Work table; Boston, Massachusetts, 1795–1810. Mahogany, white
pine; mahogany, curly maple, and satinwood veneers; silk. H: 29¾ in.,
W: 20⅞ in., D: 14⅝ in. Museum of Fine Arts, Boston. The M. and M.
Karolik Collection of 18th Century American Arts 39.166.

a poet and writer.[1] At the University of Rhode Island (URI),
from which he graduated in 1972, he majored in English and
edited the literary magazine. Yet, furniture always attracted
him: on visits to historical sites for his American literature
classes the old furniture always made the greatest impression
on him, and in his studio-art classes he made sculptures that
looked like furniture. Combining his interests in building
and in art, he rented a shop in 1970 in Saunderstown, Rhode
Island, with two other friends, a blacksmith and a leather-
worker. He borrowed tools and bought second-hand machines
to teach himself woodworking. Woodworking appealed to him
as an alternative lifestyle and a way to avoid a conventional job:
"I continued to write poetry while considering the woodworking as something creative but more practical to fall back on."[2]

By about 1972 or 1973, however, Dunnigan stopped
writing to focus on woodworking. Making kitchen cabinets,
bookcases, and a variety of furniture, much of it in a colonial
vernacular or Shaker style, satisfied his creative impulses.[3] His
close friend, Natalie Kampen, who taught classical art history
at URI, was an important influence on Dunnigan's decision to
pursue woodworking. Her career provided Dunnigan with an
example of dedication and rigorous thinking, and her schol-
arship on ancient material culture profoundly affected his
understanding of form, style, and meaning. Thus, Dunnigan's
interest in questions of design and composition developed
alongside his technical mastery.

As Dunnigan became more proficient technically and
more intrigued with design options, he sought out Tage Frid
at the Rhode Island School of Design (RISD), who counselled
against Dunnigan's entering the program, pointing out that
Dunnigan was already learning and earning more in the real
world. Later in the same year, however, Dunnigan's partnership in a shop in Wakefield, Rhode Island, dissolved, and he
was forced to take a job as a boat builder and interior cabinetmaker for the Solna Yacht Corporation in Newport. He made
some commission pieces in the evenings or on weekends in a
borrowed shop, but he did not return to full-time furnituremaking in his own shop until early 1976.

By late 1976 Dunnigan came to realize that he needed the
stimulating environment of an academic program. He had
become friends with Tim Philbrick, another Rhode Island furnituremaker who had just enrolled in the Program in Artisanry
(PIA) at Boston University. While PIA greatly impressed Dunnigan, enrolling in RISD's M.F.A. program in furniture design

Fig. b.   Table. West Kingston, Rhode Island, 1982. Wenge, purpleheart; ivoroid. H: 16 in., DIAM.: 25 in. Private collection.

Fig. c.   Desk. West Kingston, Rhode Island, 1988. Cherry, curly maple; patinated bronze. H: 29½ in., W: 58 in., D: 28½ in. Museum of Fine Arts, Boston. Gift of Anne and Ronald Abramson 1989.30.

enabled him to commute from home and keep up his own shop and home life. After one year, Frid appointed Dunnigan manager of the woodshop; this unofficial teaching position, along with his student work at RISD, validated his earlier self-taught knowledge, provided him with confidence in his empirical knowledge, and forced him to watch, understand, and teach what was being done in studio furniture.

Most of his work in the 1970s featured either steambending or laminating, and was consequently full of curves.[4] Although he has begun to feel that during this period he spent too much time making jigs, milling lumber, and wrestling with straps and clamps, Dunnigan, like other new studio furniture-makers, was all too eager to demonstrate his hard-learned technical achievements.

Since graduation in 1980, Dunnigan has continued to teach at RISD—a one-day-a-week course in furniture design or furniture history for the interior architecture and industrial design departments—and at such alternative programs as Haystack Mountain School of Crafts in Maine or Penland School in North Carolina, while maintaining a very active shop. The fresh perspective and stimulation that teaching provides prevent him from getting stale. In his recent work he blends Egyptian, Greek, and Roman inspirations to build "furniture that is technically simple, conceptually interesting and in both aspects sophisticated."

Dunnigan's work has been shown at such galleries as Pritam & Eames and Gallery Henoch, where it received wide critical acclaim. In 1982 Dunnigan was both honored by and apprehensive about his inclusion in "Masters of Woodworking," a Pritam & Eames exhibition featuring the work of Frid, George Nakashima, Sam Maloof, Wharton Esherick, Bill Keyser, Wendell Castle, Michael Coffey, Jere Osgood, and Alphonse Mattia. He decided to make a tightly designed, classically proportioned and detailed piece of furniture, but then added a twist: "I couldn't resist the temptation to make a statement about the sanctification of wood, particularly as it applied to most of the members of this group, so I added on some plastic."[5] Although traditional woodworkers viewed such a step as heresy, Dunnigan used the pink resin respectfully in detail while still honoring and respecting the integrity of the wood. It was not a joke, and attested to Dunnigan's conceptual approach to the design process, which dictates that wood is not always the best material in some places and that the use of variety in materials can effectively highlight the wood and provide visual impact. The small table (fig. b) focused Dunnigan's interest in a wide range of materials to use with wood. A recent desk of his (fig. c) combines patinated bronze accents with flaring legs that resemble Egyptian columns and routed grooves on the coved skirt that simulate corbels; mellow cherry provides overall serenity.

Dunnigan's interest in the use of other media to enrich a design has led to quite a bit of exploration and collaboration. His work in upholstery serves as a good example of his collaborative approach.[6] Since the mid-1970s he has been keenly interested in upholstery because it provides physical and visual comfort and increases the conceptual depth of a design. Dunnigan took an upholstery course in 1978, to enable himself to design upholstered furniture that better serves the needs of both upholsterer and sitter. Working with several different upholsterers over the years, Dunnigan has developed a very recognizable style: chairs with wide fronts and arms that slope down toward the back, overstuffed surfaces, and low backrests. His interest in harmonious cover fabrics has led him to collaborate with textile designers, most notably Wendy Wahl, who paints fabric with heat-set pigments. In a 1986 bench (fig. d), Wahl's hand-painted fabric covering blends perfectly with the shimmering curly maple and ebony, and the articulated, detailed extremities of Dunnigan's classical form.

Dunnigan's table (cat. 5) manifests his interest in furniture history, classical proportions and details, and combination of media.[7] Inspired by the use of fabric and gender specificity in Federal work tables (fig. a) and dressing tables, Dunnigan sought to create a new upholstered table, in which the bag served a visual, rather than a functional purpose. His choice of silk crepe, common in lingerie, reinforced the feminine quality of the form. With the pleated charmeuse silk skirt as a point of departure, he conceived of its bowed profile as the line of life for the table. He echoed this arc with a bowed apron and a top of tapered thickness. In embellishing the apron, Dunnigan reinterpreted the triglyphs and metope of classical architecture, routing out the glyphs to resemble pleated fabric and using silk-covered upholstery buttons for the metope. The texture of the glyphs and the silk lead the eye to the pleated silk skirt, and the cording along the bottom curve of the skirt flows to the cord and tassle at the leg's ankle. The thickness and stance of the elegant legs, which taper from

Fig. d. Bolster bench. West Kingston, Rhode Island, 1986. Curly maple, ebony; hand-painted silk. H: 24 in., L: 72 in., D: 24 in. Private collection.

six to four facets at the cord-embellished ankle, change as one walks around the table. Dunnigan contrasts the subtle dynamism of the table's structure to the explicit, overpowering richness of the Rhodoid, or synthetic mother-of-pearl, top.

1. Biographical information from Dunnigan's response to author's questionnaire, June 1989; and from his resume.

2. Questionnaire.

3. A 1975 ladderback chair with bent rear posts is illustrated in *Fine Woodworking Biennial Design Book* (Newtown, Conn.: Taunton Press, 1977), p. 33.

4. For examples of Dunnigan's work iduring the late 1970s, see *Fine Woodworking: Design Book Two* (Newtown, Conn.: Taunton Press, 1979), p. 81; and *Fine Woodworking: Design Book Three* (Newtown, Conn.: Taunton Press, 1983), p. 89.

5. Questionnaire.

6. For more on his upholstery work, see John Dunnigan, "Upholstered Furniture: Filling Out the Frame," *Fine Woodworking* 68 (January 1988), pp. 52–55.

7. Discussion of the table drawn from conversation with the author, June 1989.

HANK GILPIN

Fig. a. Paneled door. Shumway House, Fiskdale, Massachusetts, 1750–75. Pine. Museum of Fine Arts, Boston. Helen and Alice Colburn Fund.

6 WARDROBE
Lincoln, Rhode Island, 1989
Figured white oak, wenge
H: 56 in., W: 37¼ in., D: 16½ in.
Loaned by Hank Gilpin

Hank Gilpin (b. 1946) has achieved success making high-quality, unpretentious, and moderately priced furniture with appropriate handwork. His simple, pure understanding of wood technology and his knowledge of historical furniture have earned the respect of fellow furnituremakers and a loyal following in the New England area. His subtle design sense, meticulous workmanship, work ethic, and market awareness have made him an exemplary figure in studio furniture.

Gilpin did not begin making furniture until after graduating from Boston University.[1] He served as a photojournalist in Vietnam from 1969 to 1970, then enrolled at the Rhode Island School of Design (RISD) to do graduate work in photography. While at RISD, he took woodworking as an elective for distribution requirements and discovered a whole new means of creativity. Encouraged by Tage Frid to switch majors, Gilpin earned an M.F.A. in 1973, and apprenticed with his mentor for six months after graduation. Frid not only provided Gilpin with a solid technical foundation, but, more profoundly, established his work ethic. He emphasized the importance of activity and efficiency, and of letting the material do the work; he warned against overintellectualizing. Above all else, Frid emphasized, the furnituremaker must earn a living making furniture.

After completing his apprenticeship in December of 1973, Gilpin established his own shop in Lincoln, Rhode Island. While he took Frid's work philosophy to heart, he soon developed a very different philosophy about furniture design. While in school, he had noticed that most studio furnituremakers were interested in exploring asymmetry and curves, based particularly on Art Nouveau work; very few were working with veneer. Looking for an angle in making a living as a furnituremaker, Gilpin focused his studies on veneer work during his last year of school. After opening his own shop and struggling to establish himself as a maker of commissioned furniture, he also took on related jobs: restoration work for the RISD Museum of Art, corporate interiors, and kitchens. His willingness to tackle any sort of wood-related project allowed him to

invest his earnings back into the business and buy necessary machinery and wood, and provided him with a thorough conceptual and technical foundation. Concurrently Gilpin intensively studied the design and construction of historic furniture. He spent the summer of 1976 examining the works at the Victoria and Albert Museum in London and the Musée des Arts Décoratifs in Paris, and February of 1978 examining the furniture designed by Charles and Henry Greene in the Gamble House in Pasadena. The range of experiences and study of historical pieces provided Gilpin with empirical evidence about designs and techniques. As a result of restoration work and study, he developed an intuitive sense of practical, strong, and rich design.

Gilpin turned from veneer to hardwood in the late 1970s. He found the veneering process tedious and restrictive, and his study of historical work demonstrated that veneer was not appropriate for actively used furniture, even though, increasingly, mass-produced furniture was veneered. Gilpin switched to working in hardwood, especially domestics like white oak, maple, and cherry. He found hardwood more interesting structurally and much more enjoyable to work. At the same time, clients liked its durability and warmth. By the early 1980s Gilpin had all but abandoned other wood-related projects to focus almost exclusively on furniture.

Gilpin's method of running his shop can be summed up as follows, "Do as little as possible but work on the piece."[2] He keeps communication with clients to a minimum, spends little money on professional portfolio photography, works directly with the material and sketches using minimal full-scale working drawings, and organizes his production to make a series of one form or uses details worked out for one commission as elements in several following commissions. With two or three assistants, Gilpin is able to make between thirty-five and fifty pieces a year. Nothing is wasted—his hardwood prototypes are often sent to galleries on speculation, the money he saves not photographing each piece goes into buying wood and funding an assistant, and the time saved stocking lumber and having lumber collectors come to him allows his shop more time for production each year.

While Gilpin downplays design—to him "good design means solving the problems"[3] of practical use and affordability —through his study of historical work, he has accumulated a wealth of visual images and ideas, which he uses effectively and

with restraint. All aesthetic touches complement the function of the pieces (fig. b). As Gilpin explains, "My most necessary indulgence is merely using good wood to produce an item that is primary to the functions of daily living."[4] His shop organization, aesthetic sensibilities, and emphasis on use have allowed him to achieve success in what he identifies as the New England market—people who already own a great deal of furniture and will buy a single piece or a piece every now and then. For these clients, the product has to be functional, interesting enough to make it evocative and worth its price, and, most importantly, it must fit well in an already furnished home.

Gilpin's wardrobe (cat. 6) demonstrates his intuitive design sense based on historical work, his methods of working, and his emphasis on use. When he first saw the mid-eighteenth-century paneling from the Fiskdale House (fig. a), Gilpin immediately sensed a warmth in which purpose, materials, and technique transcended style.[5] The paneling was "high-style direct woodwork" in spite of its use in a vernacular structure: the frame stock was all of the same width and could thus be milled all at once; the panel arrangement of a square panel with long vertical panels above and below was very pleasing; the panel size kept expansion and contraction to a minimum; and the pinned mortise-and-tenon joints provided strong appropriate mechanical engineering. He chose white oak for its natural beauty and strength of character as well as its historical association: white oak has traditionally been used in woodworking of all sorts, from tools to storage vessels to furniture to buildings to bridges to ships. A lumber collector in Ohio provided him with several planks of a richly figured white oak.

With a general notion of size and detailing, Gilpin started milling his stock. He rift and quarter-cut all the leg and frame members from a single plank to create a more stable structure with uniform appearance. He then resawed other boards and bookmatched the figure of these tangential surfaces to make each pair of panels. Different sawing techniques add a subtle richness to the surface of the wardrobe. Gilpin adjusted the original size to accommodate the results of his cutting and milling. For example, a number of checks in the plank from which he cut the legs and frames prevented him from getting the full height he had planned. Rather than saw into other boards, he merely made the piece four inches shorter. Such an efficient use of wood, concern with matching figure, and confi-

focus in the field of oak, but serve a practical purpose: dirty hands opening the wardrobe will not darken the oak.

Gilpin has thus designed and built a familiar piece that is unusual in its approach to structure and form. His thorough understanding of wood, subtle decorative touches, and concern with use transcend fashion and result in a timeless work.

1. Biographical information from Gilpin's response to author's questionnaire, November 1988; and from conversations with the author, December 1988 and May 1989.

2. Quotation from Roger Holmes, "Survivors," *Fine Woodworking* 55 (November/December 1985), p. 96. Holmes provides a very good discussion of Gilpin's shop practices on pages 96 and 97.

3. *Ibid*. p. 97.

4. Quotation from Gilpin's journal chronicling the design and building of the wardrobe.

5. The discussion and analysis of the wardrobe has benefited from information from Gilpin's journal and from conversation with the author, May 1989.

Fig. b. Armchair. Lincoln, Rhode Island, 1984. Curly maple; wool. H: 33 in., W: 18 in., D: 18 in. Private collection.

dence in altering proportions demonstrates Gilpin's skill of working within the parameters of the chosen material rather than those of the preliminary drawing.

Gilpin based other elements of his design on warmth and use. He extended the panel construction completely around the carcass, permitting the wardrobe to be viewed from all sides. The gentle cant to the legs and the slight chamfering and tight fit of his panels reflect a controlled use of wood that parallels the "no-fuss, no-muss" finish. Rather than oiling or varnishing the piece, Gilpin merely planed, scraped, and wire-brushed it. Surface maintenance will consist only of a wire brushing. The wenge handles not only provide a small visual

THOMAS HUCKER

7 HIGH CHEST OF DRAWERS
Charlestown, Massachusetts, 1989
Maple, plywood, mahogany; burl aboya veneer; anodized
aluminum, black brass; black lacquer, ebonizing
H: 75½ in., W: 50½ in., D: 21 in.
Loaned by Thomas Hucker

Subtle proportion and small variations provide integral life
to the work of Thomas Hucker (b. 1955). While Eastern
aesthetics form the core of Hucker's philosophy, he combines
elements of traditional high-style European and American
furniture of the eighteenth century, Chinese furniture, and
Japanese *sukiya*-style architecture.

In the early 1970s, Hucker studied painting, sculpture,
and design at a number of schools, but a visit to the "Objects
USA" exhibition on tour in Philadelphia in 1973 focused his
interest in visual arts. Adrift in the many open-ended artistic
possibilities of the early 1970s, he found function to provide a
reassuring foundation from which to explore. In addition, furnituremaking offered the attraction of a skill to be mastered
and used.[1]

Excited by the work of Sam Maloof, Wendell Castle,
Tommy Simpson, and Jere Osgood, Hucker began to pursue
furnituremaking. In the summer of 1973, he studied with
Maloof at Penland School in North Carolina and worked in
Dan Jackson's shop. In 1974, Hucker began a two-year apprenticeship with the traditional cabinetmaker Leonard Hilgner.
The master, who had served an apprenticeship in Germany,
taught Hucker technique, discipline, and a positive self-iden-
tity based on those skills. Hucker then matriculated to Boston
University's Program in Artisanry (PIA), entering the Certificate of Mastery program in 1976. The Certificate track allowed
him to make intellectual, technical, and aesthetic progress
without the repetitions or distractions a normal undergraduate
program would have entailed. Jere Osgood had a profound
influence upon Hucker by emphasizing the joys of formal and
technical exploration and the possibilities of a quiet approach
to material manipulation. While studying with Osgood and
Alphonse Mattia at PIA, Hucker also attended the Ura Senke
School of Tea Ceremony, taught in Boston by Allen Palmer,
which introduced him to the Japanese aesthetic notion of
functional art.

Fig. a.   High chest of drawers. Boston, Massachusetts, 1700–20. Maple,
white pine, walnut; walnut and burl maple veneers. H: 63⅜ in., W: 40 in.,
D: 21⅜ in. Museum of Fine Arts, Boston. Gift of Hollis French 1940.607.

Hucker's early work manifests the sculptural influence of Dan Jackson, but his work from the late 1970s and early 1980s shows a strong Osgood and Japanese influence. His laminated curvaceous work (fig. b) was included in such museum exhibitions as "Young Americans" in 1977, "New Handmade Furniture" in 1979, and "Bentwood" in 1984; and he showed forms borrowed very directly from Japanese prototypes at Kagan Gallery, Workbench Gallery, Pritam & Eames, Snyderman Gallery, and the Society of Arts and Crafts.

The distinctive designs and formidable techniques found in Hucker's work from this period provided him many opportunities. He was commissioned to make a bench for the Museum of Fine Arts, Boston's "Please Be Seated" program (fig. c); received several private commissions; lectured at various colleges in America and Japan; taught at the Appalachian Center for Crafts in Smithville, Tennessee; was an artist-in-residence at PIA and at Tokyo University of Fine Arts, and received a National Endowment for the Arts Fellowship.[2]

Fig. b. Side chair. Boston, Massachusetts, 1976. Maple. H: 40 in., W: 23 in., D: 22 in. Private collection.

In the last five years, Hucker has entered a new phase of his career. No longer content to rely only on one-of-a-kind, gallery-oriented furniture, he has taken a greater interest in production and interior architecture. He has developed prototypes for Dansk, worked on limited runs of some forms, and has recently received a Fulbright Fellowship to attend the Domus Academy, a school in Milan, Italy, that emphasizes interior architectural design.

Accompanying Hucker's new, broader interest in design has been a loosening of his formal and aesthetic sensibilities. He has incorporated more traditional eighteenth-century features in his work, explored the variations permitted by the use of lacquered or veneered plywood, and investigated the use of such materials as bronze and steel. His close contacts with specialized shops in the Boston area have nurtured his interest in sprayed shellac or lacquer and in metalwork. For finishes he relies on Greg Johnson, and for casting and metalwork he works with David Phillips.

Hucker's high chest of drawers (cat. 7) well summarizes his new direction. Its basic form of a drawered storage unit set upon a light, turned substructure is derived from the William and Mary style popular among fashion-conscious American colonists between 1690 and 1720 (fig. a).[3] The juxtaposition of solid superstructure and skeletal substructure and the structural and visual relationships among the elements attracted Hucker. The applied cockbead molding around the carcass and drawer fronts, the shaping of the skirt, and the use of burled veneer also link his chest to the historical prototype. Hucker has incorporated these Western features within his Eastern compositional sense. A curved lacquered plywood panel cups the storage unit and provides a monolithic frame for the carcass. Hucker first used such a curtain element on a set of chairs he made for the 1986 exhibition "Craft Today: Poetry of the Physical."[4] On the high chest, the mass of the panel envelops the burl veneer and provides additional visual weight to the upper section. At the same time, the simple turnings of the legs and the arched stretchers between them emphasize the lightness of the base. The result is a very formal piece in which the facade is emphasized with a curved plane and the removal to the drawer sides of the anodized brass drawer pulls. Only the black metal pulls for the two doors break the surface.

Fig. c. Bench. Smithville, Tennessee, 1982. Beefwood; bronze. H: 16 in., W: 90 in., D: 18 in. Museum of Fine Arts, Boston. Purchased through Funds Provided by the National Endowment for the Arts, Ethan Allen, Inc., and the Robert Lehman Foundation 1982.417.

1. Biographical information from Hucker's responses to author's questionnaire, December 1988; and from his resume. Among the schools he attended between 1970 and 1975 were Pennsylvania Academy of Fine Arts, Philadelphia College of Art, Tyler School of Art, Rhode Island School of Design, University of Kansas, and Moore College of Art.

2. Additional information on these phases of Hucker's work can be found in *Language of Wood* (Buffalo, NY: Charles Burchfield Center, 1975); Tanya Barter, John Dunnigan, and Seth Stern, *Bentwood* (Providence: Museum of Art, Rhode Island School of Design, 1984), pp. 32–33; *American Craft* 44, no. 3 (June/July 1984), p. 52; and Anne Nishimura Morse and Samuel C. Morse, *Japanese Crafts/New England* (Brattleboro, VT: Brattleboro Museum & Art Center, 1987), p. 16.

3. A recent discussion of the William and Mary style, especially its emphasis on surface and form rather than ornament, is Phillip M. Johnson's "The William and Mary Style in America," in *Courts and Colonies: The William and Mary Style in Holland, England, and America* (New York: Cooper-Hewitt Museum; and Pittsburgh: The Carnegie Museum of Art, 1988), pp. 62–79.

4. Paul Smith and Edward Lucie-Smith, *Craft Today: Poetry of the Physical* (New York: American Craft Museum, 1986), p. 147.

MICHAEL HURWITZ

8 ROCKING CHAISE
Philadelphia, Pennsylvania, 1989
Mahogany; oil paint
H: 34¾ in., W: 24 in., L: 85 in.
Loaned by Michael Hurwitz

In the last ten years Michael Hurwitz (b. 1955) has drawn from a very perceptive understanding of primitive art to create furniture that blurs distinctions between actual historical forms and ideas about those forms. Like Martin Puryear, Hurwitz produces graceful work that documents "the respectful confrontation between the artist and materials," but has chosen to remain within the format of functional furniture rather than explore nonfunctional sculpture.[1]

A visit to the 1972 Renwick Gallery exhibition "Woodenworks" introduced Hurwitz to the excitement of studio furniture. Although spellbound by the magical works in that seminal show, he did not immediately pursue a career in furnituremaking. Rather he set out to become a musical-instrument maker, spending time at repair shops to pick up skills and unsuccessfully trying to secure an apprenticeship with a master craftsperson either in Boston or in Spain. In 1975, after a year at the Massachusetts College of Art in Boston, Hurwitz heard about courses in musical instrument making in the new Program in Artisanry (PIA) at Boston University. Impressed by PIA's serious commitment to the fabrication of instruments and a curriculum grounded in the traditional craft and yet part of a larger, intense craft education, Hurwitz transferred to PIA in 1975. There he studied with Don Warnoch, one of the most respected instrument makers.[2]

Although he initially enrolled at PIA to study with Warnoch, Hurwitz took furniture courses with Dan Jackson and Jere Osgood. The leadership and teaching of these two, and of Alphonse Mattia, who replaced Jackson in Hurwitz's second year, and the camaraderie among the furniture students profoundly affected Hurwitz and caused him to change majors. The interaction of teachers, older Certificate of Mastery students, and younger undergraduates created a rich sense of the physical, sensual, and cerebral aspects of furniture. As Hurwitz later remarked, he learned at PIA that wood is a medium "as capable of self-expression as any of the other traditional fine-arts media are."[3]

Hurwitz graduated from PIA in 1979 and, at the end of

Fig. a. Side chair. Samuel Gragg (1772–1855). Boston, Massachusetts, 1808–20. Oak, maple; paint. H: 34⅛ in., W: 18 in, D: 20 in. Museum of Fine Arts, Boston. Charles Hitchcock Tyler Residuary Fund 61.1074.

Fig. b.   Chairs. Cambridge, Massachusetts, 1979. Padouk; cotton velveteen. H: 48 in., W: 20 in., D: 22 in. Private collection.

Fig. c.   Bench. Philadelphia, Pennsylvania, 1986. Wenge; white latigo; milk paint. H: 18 in., W: 54 in., D: 14 in. Private collection.

that year, exhibited a tall cherry side chair (fig. b shows two of a set of six padouk chairs, for which the cherry example was the prototype) in "New Handmade Furniture" at the American Craft Museum. His chair was one of the exhibition's most frequently cited works: photographs of it appeared in *Fine Woodworking, American Craft,* and the *New York Times*.[4]

Until about 1982, Hurwitz's work was characterized by solid wood, exposed joinery, and simple though animated forms, most of which shared a concern for the relationship between design and structure.[5] In 1983, he became increasingly interested in the effects of paint and painted textures as a means of suggesting change or development of meaning over time. A fellowship in the Dominican Republic in 1985 further focused Hurwitz's interest in the honest directness of primitive art, the symbolic nature of painted textures, the beauty of abstracted nature, and the sensitive use of traditional joinery (fig. c).

Also in 1985 Hurwitz left a cooperative shop in Cambridge to assume a teaching position at the Philadelphia College of Art (PCA), now named the University of the Arts. While the cooperative had allowed him relative financial freedom to explore expressive furniture, PCA has influenced his work in a more cerebral direction. Hurwitz's approach to his designs has also changed. Although his earlier work manifested an intense interest in technical achievement, he no longer feels "compelled to invent situations for the sake of providing technical challenges."[6] He still finds wood compelling and the process of furnituremaking rewarding, but he has developed what might be considered an Eastern approach to this work: "I work because it allows me to suspend reality. I am interested as much in the activity of making as I am in the notion of producing an object."[7] Hurwitz's recent furniture blends this Eastern simplicity with quiet technical achievement and restrained design.

Hurwitz's rocking chair chaise (cat. 8) demonstrates the strength of his new work. As a PIA student he had admired many compositional aspects of a patented fancy chair by Samuel Gragg (fig. a): the scale, strength of line, relationship of positive and negative space, interplay of paint and detail, and sense of invention.[8] From the historical prototype Hurwitz excerpted such details as the continuous liquid curve of the front leg, seat rail, and rear stile; the gently rounded front seat rail; and the dovetailed joints where the seat slats fit into the front rail. Rather than recasting these elements within the same format, however, he stretched out the line and placed it upon a rocking substructure. Such an extreme scale permitted him to accentuate the light linear and curvilinear elements while also evoking an image of a magic carpet, thus becoming a vehicle of fantasy for the artist as well as the user or viewer.

In the drawing stage, Hurwitz struggled to provide his rocker with both visual and physical balance. It had to look enticing without a sitter, yet it also had to function well in a different position when a sitter rested on it. His resolution was to build a chaise form with an overscaled scrolled crest rail derived from the arm shapes of Gragg's arm chairs and set it upon a structure that evoked Japanese architecture. To achieve the desired lightness he laminated mahogany, delicately tapering the ends; to ensure strength he laminated a three-quarter-inch-square steel pipe within the two long straight horizontal pieces of the base.

Hurwitz's restrained detailing of the chaise combines both historical and personal interests. He dovetailed the seat slats into the foot and head rails and accentuated these joints by softening the inside edges of the rails and adding small wooden sprigs as a decorative touch. He then added clusters of abstracted trees or wheatsheaves between the slats that support the sitter's back. Hurwitz has used similar abstractions of plant forms as decorative structural elements in several pieces during the last four years, but here uses them to link the slats visually. With the frame constructed, Hurwitz then worked on a finish to give the piece a sense of history and meaning over time. He heavily painted it, then carefully sanded off the layers of paint to reveal some of the wood beneath.

The quiet, graceful simplicity of the chaise understates Hurwitz's refined sense of design and his technical accomplishment. He has transcended an emphasis on wood and techniques to build a fresh innovative seating form that synthesizes elements from historical works, Eastern philosophy, and contemporary needs.

1. Quotation from Hurwitz's artist statement in *The Craft Enigma* (Philadelphia: The University of the Arts, 1989), p. 22.
2. Biographical information from Hurwitz's response to author's questionnaire, January 1989; his resume; and "Michael Hurwitz," *American Craft* 46, no. 1 (February/March 1986), p. 41.
3. Questionnaire.
4. *Fine Woodworking* 18 (September/October 1979), p. 89; *American Craft* 39, no. 3 (June/July 1979), p. 11; and *New York Times*, January 3, 1980, p. C1.
5. See also *Fine Woodworking* 30 (September/October 1981), p. 94; and *Woodforms* (Brockton, Mass.: Brockton Art Museum, 1981), p. 9.
6. Questionnaire.
7. *The Craft Enigma*, p. 22.
8. Hurwitz detailed the design and construction of the chaise in a letter to the author, May 1989.

TOM LOESER

9 CHEST OF DRAWERS
New Bedford, Massachusetts, 1989
Mahogany, poplar, Baltic birch plywood, mahogany plywood;
delrin; milk paint
H: 73 in, W: 29¼ in., D: 24½ in.
Loaned by Tom Loeser

Tom Loeser (b. 1956) has been one of the leaders in the use of
paint as a compositional and decorative element. In the early
1980s, his patterned painting on high-tech forms gained him
an international reputation. His more recent work combines
milk paints and hand work to provide a rich surface that
bestows a deep emotive power to his objects. He has thus used
paint in an appropriate manner, not to overpower good workmanship or disguise shoddy work, but to work synergistically
with the wood and joinery.

Fig. a.   Chest-on-chest. Boston, Massachusetts, 1710–20. Black walnut,
Eastern white pine; walnut and burl walnut veneers. H: 70¾ in., W: 42¼
in., D: 21½ in. Museum of Fine Arts, Boston. Gift of a Friend of the
Department of American Decorative Arts and Sculpture and Otis Nor-
cross Fund 1986.240.

Loeser's introduction to the craft world was through
ceramics.[1] He had enjoyed working in that medium during
high school and worked as a thrower in a production shop
during the summer after high school. In that same summer, he
also worked as a handyman at the New England Craftsmanship Center in Watertown, Massachusetts, and began to spend
increasing amounts of time in the wood shop there. Wood
excited him because it could be used in so many different ways
and the process of building with it was engrossing. While
studying sociology and anthropology at Haverford College,
Loeser did not actively pursue woodworking, although he
worked construction in the summer and was aware of the *Fine
Woodworking* design books.

After graduating from Haverford in 1979, Loeser returned
to the Boston area and visited his old friend Mitch Ryerson,
then at Boston University's Program in Artisanry (PIA). The
work and atmosphere at PIA fascinated Loeser, who took a
summer course there, and then enrolled as a full-time student,
earning a B.A.A. in 1982. His education at PIA provided him
not only with an awareness of the inexhaustible technical
aspects of furnituremaking, but also with an ability to look
with a critical eye. Loeser's early school work tended to be of
naturally finished wood, but by the end of school he began to
use paint. The impetus for this change can be attributed to the
teaching of Alphonse Mattia and the industrial and architectural designs illustrated in magazines such as *Arbitare* and
Domus. The work of the Memphis group was particularly
important "not so much because I like the stuff, but because
it opened up the field, and made more things possible and
accepted. It combined with other things have opened people's
minds up about what furniture can be and do."[2] Loeser's work
did not imitate the Memphis work, but rather paralleled it.
Initially he used high-gloss enamel colors to provide compositional strength and unity to an upholstered, triangular chair
with deep geometric coloring.

After this foray into paint, Loeser used softer, sponged
enamels on a wall-hung folding chair designed for mass production. Made out of Baltic birch plywood with a router jig,
his chair featured an ingenious folding mechanism that
allowed the chair to function either as a seating unit or as a
decorative flat wall piece. Subsequent chairs in this series featured bolder and brighter combinations of paint. Loeser's
combination of high-tech form and colorful paint brought him

wide recognition both in America and abroad. In 1982, he won a silver medal from the Royal Society for the Encouragement of Arts, Manufactures, and Commerce in England. Loeser did not restrict his painterly interests to chairs; he also began a series of tables with black-dyed substructures reminiscent of Gerrit Rietveld's work. Interspersed as accent elements or jewels were clusters of small painted geometric shapes. The whole structure sat upon boldly painted feet.

In 1983, Loeser spent five weeks in Smithville, Tennessee, as an artist in residence at the Appalachian Center for Crafts. There he began to explore looser compositional forms and a

Fig. b.   Chest of drawers. Cambridge, Massachusetts, 1984. Yellow poplar, maple, Baltic birch plywood; ColorCore; enamel paint. H: 62 in., W: 40 in., D: 42 in. Private collection.

more informal use of paint. The glass artist Hank Adams and Wendy Maruyama, who were also in Smithville at that time, provided the impetus for this transformation. Loser worked collaboratively with Adams on a series of lamps. He also began two related series of tables—earthquake tables with legs that looked like stacked blocks and long narrow tables with tops shaped like ironing boards. Loeser pushed himself to "use unlikely shapes and forms together in a piece, trying to achieve a sense of asymmetrical and unpredicted balance. I think in terms of edges and planes, and find myself accentuating the edges of shapes again and again when I design and when I paint. I like painting on the thin edge, and the definition that the edge then gives to the larger planar surfaces."[3] In these tables of 1983 and 1984, Loeser began to use paint not so much simply to strengthen a piece's visual lines, but in a freer manner to make the work more personal. The earlier ones featured denser patterns and stronger colors, while the later examples show a more refined and controlled use of color. The patterned decoration tends to be more diffuse and the colors softer.

The chest of drawers Loeser made in 1984 for the "Material Evidence: New Techniques in Handmade Furniture" show (fig. b) is a good example of his work in the mid-1980s. It clearly demonstrates his interest in restructuring forms and using muted color to endow the piece with character.[4] Instead of building a rectilinear carcass in which drawers slid, Loeser stacked a series of separate drawer boxes within a tripod frame. He decorated each of these boxes with sponged enamel paint and covered the drawer fronts with shingles of ColorCore. He also used such shingles on the front facade through which the boxes project. The exactness of the shingles and the painstaking effort necessary to cut and fit them recalled some of the overly technical aspects of Loeser's early work, but the spokeshaven tripod elements with rubbed enamel paint and gouged drawer pulls represented his first effort at combining handwork and muted color to suggest patina.

In the past two years, Loeser has attempted to simplify his work even more. He continues to emphasize hand work, especially sawn and chiseled edges and gouged panels, to encourage more spontaneity, quicken the pace of production, and imbue the piece of furniture with character: "While I am not at all averse to using power tools, given the choice between working by hand or using power tools to accomplish the same task, I have a preference for working by hand. The actual work is more enjoyable, and I think the handworked quality shows up in the look and feel of the finished piece."[5] Careful examination of preindustrial furniture has been particularly instructive. A recent series of chests (fig. c), inspired by seventeenth-century board chests, feature sawtooth edges made with a backsaw and chisel rather than table saw jigs and fluted panels carved with gouges rather than router jigs. The gouged areas are painted with milk paint and then rubbed with steel wool, resulting in a worn patina that neatly complements the straightforward mortise-and-tenoned structural elements of the front and the butted joints of the carcass.

Loeser's recent chest of drawers (cat. 9) demonstrates how he continues to draw upon historical forms and details, but reorders them and embellishes them with carved and painted decoration.[6] Inspired by a chest-on-chest with rich surface decoration including fluted pilasters and burl veneer (fig. a), Loeser isolated the individual drawers into boxes, as he had done in his 1984 chest. He then staggered them into various planes, a compositional strategy he had used on one of his first earthquake tables. A 1928 desk and bookcase designed by Paul Frankl (1887–1958) that borrowed the setback profiles of Art Deco skyscrapers also inspired Loeser.[7] He linked these boxed drawers in a very direct manner. Instead of erecting a new supporting structure around the drawers, as he had in his 1984 chest of drawers, he merely bolted the drawer units together. On each of the units he has used gouge carving to provide rough surface decoration and to define the edges of the drawer front. From afar the gouges appear very uniform, but on closer inspection there is considerable variety in line and depth. Such variability provides the aesthetic value of what David Pye refers to as free workmanship, a conscious use of skilled unregulated work as an alternative to the highly regulated work that results in very exact and uniform surfaces.[8] Loeser uses this free-carving appropriately in conjunction with the subtle tones of milk paint. Each box features its own pairing of colors, but the gouges endow the piece with an overall unity.

Loeser's stacked drawers thus demonstrate the success of his new, simplified approach to design and construction. The work remains time-consuming and requires considerable skill, but he has created a natural simplicity of form with painted decoration that is suggestive rather than definitive.

Fig. c.   Chest over drawer. New Bedford, Massachusetts, 1989. White oak, yellow poplar, birch plywood; milk paint. H: 27 in., W: 46 in., D: 17½ in. Private collection.

1.   Biographical information from Loeser's response to author's questionnaire, January 1989; his resume; and conversations with the author, especially June 1989.

2.   Questionnaire.

3.   Loeser quoted in *Boston University Program in Artisanry Wood Department* (Philadelphia: Snyderman Gallery, 1986).

4.   The chest was illustrated in both *Material Evidence: New Color Techniques in Handmade Furniture* (Washington, D.C.: Smithsonian Institution, 1985), p. 15; and Paul Smith and Edward Lucie-Smith, *Craft Today: Poetry of the Physical* (New York: American Craft Museum, 1985), p. 152.

5.   Conversation with the author, June 1989.

6.   The discussion of the chest is based on discussion with the author, June 1989.

7.   The Frankl desk and bookcase is illustrated and discussed in Karen Davies, *At Home in Manhattan: Modern Decorative Arts, 1925 to the Depression* (New Haven: Yale University Art Gallery, 1983), pp. 68–69.

8.   David Pye, *The Nature and Art of Workmanship* (London: Cambridge University Press, 1968), esp. pp. 45–58.

KRISTINA MADSEN

10 SIDE CHAIR
Easthampton, Massachusetts, 1989
Pau ferro, maple, Baltic birch plywood; silk
H: 36¾ in., W: 19 in., D: 17 in.
Loaned by Kristina Madsen

Kristina Madsen (b. 1955) is another prominent second-generation furnituremaker who has used her mastery of traditional forms and techniques as a departure point for more personal and emotional explorations. While her superb workmanship is easily recognized, the meaning behind her final choices only becomes more apparent as one examines Madsen's career.

Madsen had no experience with wood prior to 1975.[1] In high school and college, she demonstrated an interest in and aptitude for quilting, weaving, and sewing. When, in 1975, she developed an interest in the process of woodworking, she had no awareness of contemporary studio furniture. By chance she met David Powell, an English-trained cabinetmaker working in Hatfield, Massachusetts, and began to study with him independently. Powell's expertise in the use of hand tools provided Madsen with an extremely solid traditional technical foundation. His restrained, conservative design sense also had a profound impact upon her: she developed a strong intuitive design sense with which she could surpass her teacher's work.

Madsen studied with Powell for two years before enrolling, in 1977, in his newly established Leeds Design Workshop, an alternative to the academic training programs at colleges and universities. After two years as a student, she stayed on as an instructor at Leeds for five years. During her time at Leeds, Madsen incorporated such power tools as routers and shapers into her technical repertoire and gained greater awareness of the expanding field of American studio furniture. From 1984 through the fall of 1988, she worked in a cooperative shop in the Leeds building with three furnituremakers who had studied with or worked for Wendell Castle: Silas Kopf, Bruce Volz, and Wendy Stayman. In late 1988, she set up a shop with furnituremaker John Clark. Her education has thus been a combination of private lessons, formal training, and informal sharing with colleagues.

Madsen has gradually emerged as one of the leading American furnituremakers: she gained her first public exposure at a 1979 exhibition of Massachusetts crafts at the

Fig. a.   Side chair. Philadelphia, Pennsylvania, 1795–1810. Beech, maple, pine; paint. H: 38¾ in., W: 21¾ in., D: 19 in. Museum of Fine Arts, Boston. M. and M. Karolik Collection of 18th Century American Arts 39.108.

Fig. b. Bench. Easthampton, Massachusetts, 1988. Tasmanian myrtle. H: 11 in., W: 40 in., D: 10½ in. Private collection.

Danforth Museum. Steadily increasing recognition followed: she was awarded a NEA Fellowship in 1980, participated in the 1981 exhibition "Woodforms" at the Brockton Art Museum,[2] and subsequently has shown work in such galleries as Workbench, Pritam & Eames, Snyderman, and Bernice Steinbaum.

Accompanying Madsen's increased exhibition presence was a maturing of her own design sense. Much of her earlier work relates to the refined designs of Powell and the British cabinetmaker Edward Barnsley, with whom Powell apprenticed. But in 1984 she began to incorporate richly textured and varied surface decoration in her work. Inspired by the carved work in Roland and Maryanne Force's *The Fuller Collection of Pacific Artifacts*,[3] especially the Maori and Fijian clubs with geometric patterns of gouged grooves, Madsen began to

experiment with achieving a similar textural depth with routed grooves. She routed out grooves on a board, then cut up the board and reassembled the pieces to establish different rhythms or patterns. Using modern technology, she has reinterpreted the textures of the confident, "free workmanship" of the South Pacific (fig. b).[4]

A second stage in Madsen's emergence was a 1986 show at the Workbench Gallery, entitled "Masterpieces." This thematic show featured furniture inspired by objects depicted in paintings. For this show, Madsen made *Bird's Nest Chair* (fig. c), an oval-back chair taken from Remedios Varo's "Harmony," painted in 1956. Eager to try her hand at a semi-functional work and to incorporate the visual warmth and richness of upholstery into her work, Madsen responded to the fine lines of the legs and the oval back. Her interest in upholstery also harkened back to her earlier efforts in quilting and sewing. Since making *Bird's Nest Chair*, she has simplified her forms and focused her attention on providing decorative variety and depth.

Madsen was artist-in-residence at the University of Tasmania School of Art in Australia for four months in 1988. While in the South Pacific, she saw an exhibition of New Guinea artifacts in Sydney and visited with carvers who carried on the Maori carving traditions. The ease of their carving, the beauty of their graphic patterns, and the levels of meaning in their patterns inspired Madsen.

Madsen's oval-back chair (cat. 10) demonstrates the continuing development of her own personal style.[5] Recalling her fondness for her own *Bird's Nest Chair*, Madsen responded to the beauty of a Philadelphia chair (fig. a), and decided to make an oval-back chair that was more functional than her earlier work, but still had some depth of meaning. She borrowed the elegance of the back, but then emphasized this rounded elegance by using turned front and rear legs. To provide surface texture, she routed grooves into the seat rails. While the shape of the upholstered back is derived directly from that of a paddle club that she brought back from the South Pacific, this back is not carved. Madsen's use of fabric gives the work a different emotional meaning. The padding provides comfort, the blue silk endows the chair with a rich texture, and the piping in the back and along the edge of the seat offers a personal accent.

Madsen's designs of the late 1980s demonstrate that she has transcended her reputation as a "cabinetmaker par excellence."[6] Her work's quiet thoughtfulness is achieved through subtle manipulation of materials, textures, and lines. A description of Papua, New Guinea, carvers articulates well Madsen's own South Pacific-based philosophy: "The master carver has more than just technical skills. He has qualities known as *sope*; his work flows freely and naturally like water. He has *migila*, by which magical qualities are transferred to the carving, and *kakapisi*, the ability to arouse emotions of sadness and happiness in those who see his work. His carvings have clean, pure lines and a balance of color that bring charm and beauty. He is an innovator who never makes two identical pieces."[7]

Fig. c.   *Bird's Nest Chair.* Easthampton, Massachusetts, 1986. Pau ferro; sueded pigskin. H: 39 in., W: 14 in., D: 16 in. Private collection.

1. Biographical information drawn from response to the author's questionnaire, February 1989; her resume; and an interview with the author, December 1988.

2. A pair of simple music stands was illustrated on p. 12 of *Woodforms* (Brockton, Mass: Brockton Art Museum, 1981).

3. New York: Praeger, 1971.

4. The term "free workmanship," to describe sure unregulated craft work is taken from David Pye, *The Nature and Art of Workmanship* (London: Cambridge University Press, 1968), esp. pp. 45–58.

5. Conversation with the author, April 1989.

6. Nina Stritzler, *Pioneer & Pioneering Women in 20th Century Furniture Designers & Furniture Designer/Makers* (New York: Bernice Steinbaum Gallery, 1988), p. 9.

7. Quotation from an exhibition label at the Sydney Museum, supplied by Madsen.

WENDY MARUYAMA

Fig. a   High chest. Philadelphia, Pennsylvania, 1760–80. Mahogany, pine, yellow poplar; mahogany veneer. H: 93 in., W: 43 in., D: 23 in. Museum of Fine Arts, Boston. M. and M. Karolik Collection of American Arts 1939.545.

11 HIGH CHEST
Oakland, California, 1989
Mahogany, maple, basswood; copper leaf; casein paints
H: 84 in., W: 40¾ in., D: 21¼ in.
Loaned by Wendy Maruyama

Wendy Maruyama (b. 1952) is constantly testing the limits of conventional furniture. She has combined a training in traditional techniques with a commitment to sculptural shapes, painted surfaces, and expressive content. Maruyama explains her own philosophy succinctly, "I consider myself an artist who makes furniture or furniture-related objects."[1] Her work satirizes "what furniture is and has always been" and questions why "couldn't it be something else."[2]

Maruyama discovered woodworking in the late 1960s, when craft programs were expanding throughout the country.[3] In a multimedia craft class at Southwestern Junior College, she made a three-legged chair and developed a special interest in furniture. Woodworking appealed to her because she had originally viewed it as something in which only males could gain proficiency. Maruyama transferred to San Diego State University to study with Lawrence Hunter, a prominent West Coast woodworker best known for his stack-laminated work. She closely imitated Hunter's own work, building massive organically shaped stacked forms, which she decorated with such materials as beads, fur, and feathers. However, the slides Hunter showed in class and the books he assigned also introduced her to woodworking throughout the country and broadened her perspective. Especially taken with the work of Wendell Castle and Tommy Simpson, Maruyama began to see the "great potential of furniture as an art form." Carefully watching the work on the East Coast, Maruyama soon began to admire especially the work of Dan Jackson and Alphonse Mattia, who used traditional techniques in a more sophisticated and expressive manner.

After graduating in 1975, to improve her technical skills, she enrolled at Virginia Commonwealth University (VCU), where Mattia was teaching. Her one semester there was a rude shock. Her previous technical repertoire had been limited to stack lamination and doweling; the sheer variety of other techniques, and the precision demanded by dovetails, mortise-and-tenon joints, and bridle joints overwhelmed her. Maruyama left VCU, and enrolled in 1976 in a two-year course of study at

Fig. b. *Striped Pinto*. Smithville, Tennessee, 1982. Plywood; glass; enamel paint. H: 18 in., W: 24 in., D: 36 in. Private collection.

Boston University's Program in Artisanry (PIA), where Mattia had just begun teaching. Encouraged by Osgood and Mattia and by the camaraderie among the students, Maruyama went beyond her early, self-conscious work and built a body of fairly traditional works in order to master the conventional techniques. The intensity of the program and the quality of students and faculty not only provided her with a solid technical base and a better developed sense of composition and design, but affirmed her commitment to the field.

From PIA, Maruyama went on to the Rochester Institute of Technology (RIT), earning an M.F.A. in 1980. The conservative environment at RIT galvanized her ideas about expressive furniture, and in her second year she began to paint her furniture and use unconventional shapes (fig. b). While the criticism at RIT strengthened Maruyama, Castle and the Memphis group provided inspiration. The former's furniture in the Art Deco style and professional presentation provided new standards of quality for the field, while the latter legitimized a more relaxed approach to concept. For Maruyama, the Mem-

phis work "eliminated the fear of doing timely or trendy work simply for the fun and need to express something."[4]

Maruyama's work since 1980 demonstrates the influence of this freedom. Not confined by a particular aesthetic, she tends to produce a block of interrelated work and then to move to another block. In 1980 and 1981, she worked in a very angular, rectilinear style using a variety of media—including metal, glass, and colored epoxies—focusing upon freehand painted surfaces for decoration. Throughout this work, she used color to define form, provide decorative imagery, and convey energy.[5]

By 1984 Maruyama grew tired of painting and its widespread popularity in the furniture field. Seeking to establish her own niche, she embarked upon a "white period," in which she bleached everything or simply painted it white. The bleaching, which removed the color while retaining its natural surface, was accompanied by a simplification of form. She referred to her bare-bones, bare-color furniture as "post-nuclear primitive," a statement against the effects of nuclear arms (fig. c). She imagined that such a style would emerge "if the world were to survive a nuclear war and re-evolve . . . and start designing furniture again. The forms would be very stark; the wood will have lost its color."[6] For the 1984 "Material Evidence: New Color Techniques in Handmade Furniture" exhibition at the Workbench Gallery and the Renwick Gallery and the 1986 "Craft Today: Poetry of the Physical" exhibition at the American Craft Museum, Maruyama adapted her post-nuclear primitive style slightly. She used stark forms, bleached wood, and very light ColorCore, but added some architectural detailing.

Maruyama's white phase ran its course by about 1986, when she returned to organic shapes and painted surfaces. But she combined these features with a traditional approach to functional, rectilinear forms: benches with very flat rectangular surfaces, cabinets with rectangular shelved storage areas behind doors, and chests with stacked drawers. This functional core is painted with subtle tonal gradations with incised contrasts and then screened or enhanced by rounded fins, bamboolike turned spindles, or neon lights. Her use of a surform and casein paints to provide textural color complements the slightly softened pods or fins she uses for legs and pillars.

Maruyama has divided her time about equally between furnituremaking and teaching. One or two part-time assistants help her maintain her blend of speculative gallery work and commission work. Since 1981 her work has been shown in a wide number of shows, ranging from such museum exhibitions as "Material Evidence: New Color Techniques in Handmade Furniture" and "Craft Today: Poetry of the Physical," to gallery shows at Esther Saks in Chicago and Rena Bransten in San Francisco, to public expositions at the San Francisco International Airport. The consistent quality of her artistic explorations has earned her three fellowships from the National Endowment for the Arts and one from the Tennessee Arts Commission when she taught at the Appalachian Center for Crafts. From 1985 to 1989 she headed the Woodworking and Furniture Design Program at the California College of Arts and Crafts, and just recently accepted a similar position at her alma mater, San Diego State University.

Maruyama's high chest (cat. 11) manifests her current interest in traditional function surrounded by rounded painted forms and surformed textures. Inspired by the sculptural monumentality of a Philadelphia high chest (fig. a), she recast the massing within her own composition and aesthetic. She retained a lower drawered-section, but set it within, rather than above, the four legs. The painted and textured surface of these fin legs, echoed by a similar treatment on the drawer pulls, typifies Maruyama's contrast of softened decorative details and rectilinearity. Her treatment of the upper section emphasizes this approach. She minimized the upper section by making it a shelved space with doors and then emphasized the decorative elements with greater size, purple paint, and copper leaf. Maruyama describes the central pyramid and flanking pods as finials since they serve the same iconological function as the cartouche and flame finials on the Philadelphia example.

By exaggerating traditional forms, adding new energetic elements, and balancing hard and soft lines, Maruyama has achieved a different kind of sculptural monumentality. Whereas the Philadelphia cabinetmaker used width in the lower section, height in the upper section, and an emphasis on the figured and carved front facade to provide a well-contained vertical thrust, Maruyama's subtly toned carcass minimizes the functional mass, and a richly decorated series of appendages provide a three-dimensional outward thrust.

Fig. c. *Post-Nuclear Primitive*. Oakland, California, 1986. Cherry. H: 48 in., W: 15 in., D: 17 in. Private collection.

1. Maruyama quoted in Denise Domergue, *Artists Design Furniture* (New York: Harry Abrams, 1984), p.117.

2. Maruyama quoted in Terrie Noll, "Finding Your Own Voice," *Woodwork* 1 (spring 1989), p. 40.

3. Biographical information from Domergue; Noll; Maruyama's responses to author's questionnaire, December 1988; and from her resume.

4. Questionnaire.

5. See "Portfolio: Wendy Maruyama", *American Craft* 41, no. 5 (October/November 1981), p.44.

6. Noll, p. 40; and questionnaire.

7. *Material Evidence: New Color Techniques in Handmade Furniture* (Washington, D.C.: Smithsonian Institution, 1985), p. 14; and Paul Smith and Edward Lucie-Smith, *Craft Today: Poetry of the Physical* (New York: American Craft Museum, 1986), p. 156.

ALPHONSE MATTIA

12 PAIR OF EASY CHAIRS
Westport, Massachusetts, 1989
Soft curly maple, ash; knitted wool; milk paint
Upholstered by Aarne Read
H: 49½ in., W: 36 in., D: 31½ in.
Loaned by Alphonse Mattia

Through his work and teaching, Alphonse Mattia (b. 1947) has exerted immense influence on the second generation of American studio furnituremakers. He has continually resisted the accepted rules for furniture, producing a body of very sculptural, quasi-functional furniture, yet also making very designed pieces of functional furniture. His eclectic approach relates all work to its cultural environment. Mattia allows his imagination or emotions to transform the traditional respect for wood, woodworking techniques, and furniture history into new and vibrant three-dimensional forms: "I try to ground my work in the context of familiarity. . . . Once the familiar connection is established, anything goes."[1]

Fig. a.   Easy chair. Boston, Massachusetts, 1705–20. Maple, white pine; reproduction worsted wool cover. H: 48¾ in., W: 29⅛ in., D: 24 in. Museum of Fine Arts, Boston. Gift of Robert L. Parker and Margaret S. Parker in Memory of Winifred Franklin Jones 1976.727.

As a child, Mattia made wooden objects in a basement shop with his father, who was trained in Italy as a carpenter and cabinetmaker, but Mattia spent most of his creative energy customizing plastic model cars.[2] During high school he helped to design and construct displays for a neighborhood hobby store, whose owners suggested he attend art school. He chose Philadelphia College of Art with the intention of majoring in industrial design, but after discovering the wood studio in the dimensional design department, he decided to major in wood. Studying with Dan Jackson, Mattia learned to look at and understand a wide range of furniture, from antique to Art Nouveau to Scandinavian Modern; use appropriate cabinetmaking techniques and produce functional work; and make voluptuous work that is original, personal, and contemporary.[3] After graduation, Mattia worked for Jackson and then rented space from Jackson's assistant Bob Worth. While the swelling shapes, exposed joinery—particularly through-mortises made with horizontal mortisers—, and considerable attention to shaping and carving of Mattia's furniture of the period resembled his teacher's work, he was developing his own less organic expressive style.

In 1971, Mattia entered the Rhode Island School of Design (RISD) in order to study with Tage Frid, whose positive outlook, sense of humor, and gregarious nature, as well as his more linear approach to design helped Mattia further refine his own direction. Mattia continued to lighten up some of the structural elements and expanded his technical repertoire to include tambour, veneer, and upholstery.

After receiving his M.F.A. from RISD in 1973, Mattia taught at Virginia Commonwealth University until 1976, when Boston University recruited him to teach at the Program in Artisanry (PIA) with Jere Osgood. He has remained a professor of woodworking and furniture design as PIA first moved to the Swain School of Design in New Bedford, Massachusetts, and then was absorbed by Southeastern Massachusetts University. His personal approach, broad technical knowledge, and keen interest in incorporating contemporary culture and traditional furnituremaking techniques has inspired many PIA students.

By 1979, however, Mattia had become frustrated by studio furnituremakers' reluctance to take advantage of the expressive possibilities of color, as contemporary industrial designers, ceramists, and craftspeople in other media were doing. He

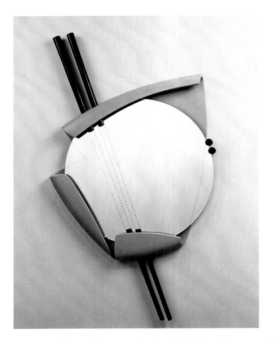

Fig. b. *Chopsticks Mirror*. Roslindale, Massachusetts, 1980. Burl sedua, Baltic birch plywood; mirror glass; enamel paint. H: 52 in., W: 24 in., D: 4½ in. Private collection.

wanted to work in a more sculptural fashion that was "related to function, but not ruled by it."[4] He also wanted to work on a related series of objects in order to more deeply explore an idea or a form rather than making one or two pieces for a show or commission and then starting all over again with a new set of parameters. He stopped making furniture and instead made a series of wall mirrors that involved carving, shaping, and paint (fig. b). He even sandblasted through the glass and painted lines to suggest hidden structure and to personalize a commercially available part of the mirror.[5]

The series of mirrors and a subsequent commission for a wall sculpture based upon the mirrors allowed Mattia to reenergize his work and push the boundaries of traditional furniture to focus on line, form, color, texture, and literal images. He began to work along two different tracks: serious design and graphic humor. In the former he explored forms and decoration with very severe geometry, often using paint to play off of its harshness. For a dining table commission (fig. c), he used

the geometry of a triangle as an organizing motif, both structurally and decoratively. At the same time he made a series of tables and chairs that incorporated triangles in various ways: low tables that used hollow triangular tubes for the top surface; tables with triangulated cross pieces underneath glass tops with triangular decoration; and chairs whose legs had triangular cross-sections, triangular patterns of wood on the back, and triangular inlays on the front rails.

Mattia's humor is best seen in a series of valets inspired by valets designed in the early 1950s by the noted Danish cabinetmaker Hans Wegner. Preserving the basic structure of the form—the low seat that eases shoe tieing and the hanging supports for coats, ties, or other clothing—Mattia used paint, shaping, and carved elements to make his valets playful and animated (fig. d). Mattia's valets have been featured in the 1984 "Bentwood" exhibition at the RISD Museum of Art and the 1986 "Craft Today: Poetry of the Physical" exhibition at the American Craft Museum; and examples have been purchased for the permanent collections of the Museum of Fine Arts, Boston, the Rhode Island School of Design Museum of Art, and the Yale University Art Gallery.[6]

Whether working in a more designerly or more humorous mode, Mattia believes furniture, "while playing with our feelings and memories, should expand and redefine our notions

Fig. c. Dining table. Roslindale, Massachusetts, 1984. Wenge, cherry, holly. H: 29 in., W: 43 in., L: 86 in. Private collection.

about objects."[7] He sketches profusely to generate ideas and work out options and then turns to a variety of techniques: "I enjoy the machinework but not as much as shaping and carving."[8]

In drawing inspiration from the Museum of Fine Arts collection, Mattia focused upon the easy chair form to design a "quasi-traditional" pair that reflects the evolutionary nature of the form (cat. 12). Inspired by an early eighteenth-century example (fig. a), he sought to explore the "reversing, inverting, and evolving of the scrolls and the subtle variations and interpretations of the design."[9] He was intrigued in particular by the vertical orientation of the C-scrolls of the arms in the early examples and the horizontal orientation on later Philadelphia examples. Mattia also built two chairs—one fully upholstered and one frame—because books and museum installations often show both, and because he feels that the understructure of an upholstered chair is crucial to its form. He made each chair asymmetrical apart, but bilaterally symmetrical when used together; he enlarged the wing element in order to control access to the sitter and to provide visual variety rather than to provide comfort by sheltering the sitter from drafts; and he sought to offer a substructure that was more than just four legs.

Since 1973 Mattia has been drawn to the volumetric, formal possibilities of upholstered furniture. Part of this interest stemmed from Jackson's influence; Mattia attributed to his teacher the "heavy, juicy shaping and elegant linear profiles" of his most recent easy chair. Another catalyst in Mattia's exploration of upholstered furniture has been the sculpture of Paul Harris, who used his training as an upholsterer's apprentice in his later art work, melding trade experience and art ideas as H.C. Westermann had. Unlike Mattia's easy chair of 1976, which has only a small cherry molding along the bottom edge of a velour-covered frame, the recent piece uses wood, fabric, and stuffing in equal parts to address issues of form, texture, and history.[10]

Fig. d. *Brains*. Roslindale, Massachusetts, 1983. Poplar; analine dye and enamel paint. H: 65 in., W: 20 in., D: 20 in. Private collection.

1. Joy Cattanach Smith, "Furniture: A Sculptural Medium," *Art New England* 7, no. 1 (December/January 1985–86), p. 4.

2. Biographical information from Smith; Mattia's response to author's questionnaire, June 1989; Mattia's resume; and numerous conversations with the author.

3. See Franklin Parrasch, *A Tribute to Daniel Jackson* (Washington, D.C.: Franklin Parrasch Gallery, 1989).

4. Smith, p. 4.

5. For a discussion of this series, see *Woodforms* (Brockton, Mass.: Brockton Art Museum, 1981), p. 14.

6. Tanya Barter, John Dunnigan, and Seth Stem, *Bentwood* (Providence, RI: Museum of Art, Rhode Island School of Design, 1984), pp. 40–41; and Paul Smith and Edward Lucie-Smith, *Craft Today: Poetry of the Physical* (New York: American Craft Museum, 1986), p. 135.

7. Barter, Dunnigan, and Stem, p. 40.

8. Smith, p. 4.

9. Discussion of the pair of chairs is drawn from discussions with the author, June 1989, and from his sketchbook.

10. The 1976 chair is illustrated in *Fine Woodworking* 14 (January/ February 1979), p. 60.

JUDY KENSLEY McKIE

13 LEOPARD CHEST
Cambridge, Massachusetts, 1989
Basswood; oil paint, gold leaf
H: 33⅜ in., W: 49⅞ in., D: 18 in.
Loaned by Judy Kensley McKie

The furniture of Judy Kensley McKie (b. 1944) is known for its elegant primitivism. Stylized flora and fauna imbue her works with animation and personality, permitting flights of imagination, evoking humor, or providing thoughtful entertainment. Emphasizing the importance of image and idea in her work, McKie explains, "I think first of the image. The craftsmanship and function are integrated in the work, but I don't think they are more important than the idea."[1]

McKie developed her practical approach to the visual arts shortly after graduation from the Rhode Island School of Design in 1966. Although trained as a painter, she came to see the painting as a self-indulgent exercise, and had difficulty justifying the time spent on producing nonfunctional works. She missed the sense of accomplishment she had enjoyed as an adolescent helping her family renovate an old boat house and, later, making furniture for her husband Todd and herself in the late 1960s, when they supported themselves by making appliqued wall hangings.

Fig. a. Chest. Charles Prendergast (1869–1948). New York City, 1927. Pine; gesso, tempera, gold leaf. H: 19⅝ in., W: 51¾ in., D: 19¼ in.. Museum of Fine Arts, Boston. John H. and Ernestine A. Payne Fund 67.732.

McKie's enjoyment of the furnituremaking process led her to change careers in 1971, and rent space in the New Hamburger Cabinetworks cooperative, located first in Roxbury and later in Cambridgeport. Most members of the cooperative were idealistic graduates of liberal arts colleges who sought alternative careers in carpentry, renovation, cabinetry, and millwork. McKie gained a living by doing finish carpentry and making straightforward, simple, and unadorned birch plywood furniture in what she refers to as "Design Research style." With Ernest Joyce's *Encyclopedia of Furnituremaking* as her bible, she learned from trial and error, benefitting also from the machinery and insights of the other members of the shop.[2]

Dissatisfied with her well-designed modern forms and concerned that she had become a mere technician capable of making only cold, impersonal work derived from an automatic design process, McKie began in 1975 to explore ways in which she could endow her work with personal care and vitality. She returned to drawing to gain inspiration. In drawing curves and images of living things, McKie gained respect for the effortless appearance, lack of superfluous ornament, and individuality of primitive work. She found the work of Pre-Columbian, African, and Native American cultures to be especially powerful and sophisticated.

By 1977 McKie had begun to employ animal imagery that was ambiguous rather than realistic to bestow a level of magic and mystery to her work. At first she merely carved such graphic images upon plain boxes (fig. b), but she soon began to carve animalistic structural members (fig. c). In 1979 she started to paint some of her carved pieces to reinforce the primitive aspect of her work. Working in palettes that resembled ancient earthenware pottery or porcelain clays, McKie experimented with painted effects. In some work she thought to evoke an ancient feeling, in others to make wood look like porcelain, and in others to make a simple form look more complex.

It proved a critical year for McKie in several ways. Three of her pieces were included in "New Handmade Furniture" at the American Craft Museum; the Museum of Fine Arts, Boston, commissioned a bench for its "Please Be Seated" program of public gallery seating; and the National Endowment for the Arts awarded her a Craftsman's Fellowship. The museum pieces brought her work to the attention of a wide audience and resulted in a steady series of commissions. The

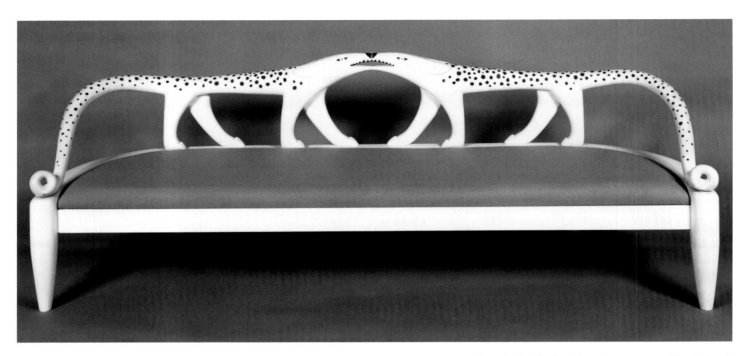

Fig. b.   Frog box. Cambridge, Massachusetts, 1975. Pine. H: 3 in., W: 8½ in., D: 5½ in. Private collection.

Fig. c.   Leopard couch. Cambridge, Massachusetts, 1983. Bleached and burned mahogany. H: 30½ in., W: 90 in., D: 25 in. Collection of Frances and Sidney Lewis.

NEA fellowship, which she received again in 1982, allowed her to purchase new equipment and to explore new ideas without the pressure of sales.

Since 1979 McKie has explored many different decorative avenues—carved forms of such unfigured works as poplar or basswood (see fig. b), carved and painted sculptural elements (see fig. c), marquetry panels of different colored woods (see fig. d). She has even translated her wooden work into bronze. Her interest in depicting imaginary animals has remained a common theme.

McKie's training in painting provided her an important foundation in how to look and how to think visually. Her work since 1977 has drawn on this skill and a reliance upon working out ideas in sketch form. In making a piece, she begins by sketching a variety of loose images that represent new abstractions or syntheses of animals or plants. During this initial phase she explores shape, proportions, and color in order to work up a successful and interesting idea. With the idea refined, she then adapts the image to a furniture form, whether as a graphic decorative device or a structural element. Finally she determines the simplest, most appropriate joinery to execute the idea and the form. She shuns a dogmatic approach to technique but chooses the most efficient construction to produce the desired effect. As a result she usually relies upon traditional construction, although she has made bent-laminated pieces. Similarly she appreciates the inherent qualities of wood and its ability to make personal statements, but does not confine herself to natural wood only.

While striving for a personal approach to furniture, McKie is pragmatic in the organization of her shop. She makes cost-effective use of her design and production time by producing most of her designs in multiple. She sends prototypes of her carved structural work to a shop with a double carving machine for duplication, and finishes the carving by hand. McKie also hires other craftspeople to make carcasses and rough some pieces out, following her drawings.

McKie's most recent chest (cat. 13) further explores her animalistic imagery within a new formal and decorative format. The inspiration was a chest by the American artist and framemaker Charles Prendergast (1868–1948). His use of carving in conjunction with gesso elements, incised painted designs, and burnished gold leaf accents (fig. a) sparked McKie, who shares Prendergast's interest in the decorative expression of whimsy and mystery. Contemporary critics called Prendergast "a true primitive" who takes us to "a world where almost anything might happen, except the commonplace"; the same might be said of McKie's work.[3] Inspired by elements of Prendergast's surface decoration, she developed a design with leopard-like animals that continue around the four sides and decorate both sides of the top.

McKie drew up her designs, had another furnituremaker make the carcass, and then began her work. She carved the basswood panels, then applied layers of shellac, Japanned boule, and paint. Along the stiles and rails she rubbed the paint with cotton to imitate the natural aging of the inspirational piece. She then gold leafed, burnished, and rubbed the leopards. To develop her color palette and try her hand at goldleafing, McKie first experimented with handmade paper panels at the Rugg Road Studio in Somerville, Massachusetts. She has been using papermaking as an adjunct to furniture-making for the past three years. While other furnituremakers depend upon full-scale drawings, McKie finds them lacking in spontaneity, an essential characteristic of her personal style. Making paper constructions enabled her to experiment with color, texture, and gold leaf.

For the past several summers, McKie and her husband have lived in Sante Fe. McKie's interest in Native American

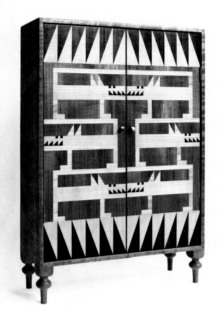

Fig. d.   Jewelry cabinet with dogs. Cambridge, Massachusetts, 1976. Cherry; walnut, maple, and teak marquetry. H: 29 in., W: 19 in., D: 7 in. Private collection.

and Colonial Spanish material culture is reflected in the earthenware-colored field of the panels and the burnished effect of the black framing members, which recall the pottery of the pueblos, and in the stepped profile of the knee-brackets, which resembles those of Spanish chests.

1.   Quotation from conversation with the author, June 1989.
2.   McKie's response to author's questionnaire, December 1988. Other sources of biographical information on McKie are Alphonse Mattia, "Judy Kensley McKie," The Workshop 2 (Summer 1983), pp. 10–12; Joy Cattanach Smith, "Judy Kensley McKie," American Craft 43, no. 6 (December 1983/January 1984), pp. 2–6; Judy Kensley McKie, "Portfolio: Judy Kensley McKie," Fine Woodworking 44 (January/ February 1984), pp. 76–81; Denise Domergue, Furniture by Artists (New York: Harry Abrams, 1984), pp. 120–21; and Lois Tarlow, "Judy Kensley McKie" Art New England 8, no. 5 (May 1987), pp. 10–11 and 26.
3.   Quotation is taken from Suzanne LaFollette's review of Prendergast's work in Art in America in 1929, as transcribed in The Prendergasts (Andover, Mass.: Addison Gallery of American Art, 1938), p. 51.

RICHARD SCOTT NEWMAN

14 COMMODE
Rochester, New York, 1989
Mahogany, cherry, yellow poplar, pearwood, ebony; curly
maple, pearwood, ebony veneers; brass
H: 35½ in., W: 46 in., D: 20 in.
Loaned by Richard Scott Newman

Since the early 1970s, Richard Scott Newman (b. 1946) has
pursued alternatives to the shocking, bold, and provocative
postures of Modernism. Recognizing that daily life possesses
enough of these qualities, he has focused his creative energies
upon graceful, elegant objects intended to provide comfort
and delight. Trained in the organic, antihistorical style of Wendell Castle, Newman developed his alternative approach by
making banjos in the 1970s, and reached full maturity by making neoclassically inspired furniture in the 1980s.

As a teenager, Newman demonstrated academic aptitude
in science and a fondness for playing the banjo.[1] He entered
Cornell at sixteen, intending to major in physics and engineering. After two years, he took a leave of absence to make banjos
or guitars, which he had begun to design and build while at
Cornell. He found no jobs making those instruments, but did
accept a six-month job at the Sohner piano factory in New
York City. There he worked with traditionally trained German
and Italian craftspeople, seeing firsthand the discipline, standards, and workmanship of master artisans and yet also recognizing the tedium of such repetitive work. While working at
the piano factory, Newman was introduced to studio furniture
—a 1964 exhibition at the Museum of Contemporary Crafts
that included work by Sam Maloof, Tommy Simpson, and
Wendell Castle. Newman found the work exciting and original
and felt that furniture had the potential to sustain his interest
longer than musical instruments. When he returned to Cornell, he sought to transfer to Cornell's art school. However, the
dean of the art school considered his interest in wood and
musical instruments inappropriate.

To pursue furnituremaking, Newman applied in 1966 to
the Rochester Institute of Technology (RIT), the only four-year
college-degree program. RIT also appealed to him because
Castle taught there. After just one year, he left school to work
three days a week as Castle's ''sand monkey''—an assistant
who prepares boards, and does some joinery, but primarily
scrapes and sands—and to gain more practical experience and

Fig. a.   Commode. Thomas Seymour. Boston, Massachusetts, 1809.
Mahogany, white pine, maple, chesnut; bird's-eye maple, mahogany, satin-
wood veneers; brass. H: 41½ in., W: 50 in., D: 24⅝ in. Museum of Fine
Arts, Boston. Gift of Martha Codman 23.19.

develop his own commission work. His work of this period (fig. b. was conceived at this time, but assembled later) merged the muscular swelling of stack-laminated work with conventional cabinetmaking techniques. His use of dovetailed carcasses, coopered doors, and spokeshaven surfaces made him appreciate the work of James Krenov, who came to teach at RIT in 1969. Krenov's poetic approach to traditional techniques lured Newman back to RIT: he eventually graduated in 1973. Krenov's respect for wood and the sophisticated technical approach of Jere Osgood, who taught at RIT from 1971 until 1975, helped to shape Newman's own developing approach. He began to realize that the work of the late 1960s "lacked sophistication and complexity when compared to the masterpieces of the past. I guess I always thought we were making a sort of folk art really."[2]

While finishing up at RIT, Newman worked for interior designers, producing slick, veneered furniture in Ruhlmann or Deco styles for the local market. He enjoyed the challenge of making sophisticated work with seamless veneered curves, developing a thermo-pneumatic process to achieve this end. As he explained it, "I have always been interested in coaxing wood, which is essentially a stiff linear material, into interesting curves. I've also been drawn to apply veneers to sculptural forms."[3]

In the 1970s Newman also devoted considerable attention to designing and building banjos. Studying a turn-of-the-century Fairbanks and the technical processes involved in making it, he began to make subtle changes that resulted in a new work that remained true to the period feeling. This connection to a tradition proved a turning point for Newman, who poured his soul into the work and worked fourteen-hour days feeling possessed by the spirit of an old banjo maker: "It was wonderful having a solid tradition to plug into and from which to evolve in a relaxed and natural way, as opposed to the self-conscious forced innovation so prevalent in much modern furnituremaking."[4] With Ken Parker, a metalworker who had previously been a machinist, Newman made richly embellished banjos that were highly praised by musicians for their exquisite sound and stylish looks (fig. c).

A 1981 commission provided Newman the opportunity to integrate traditional form and ornate decoration—inlay, carving, metal casting and engraving, and use of contrasting woods—into his furnituremaking. His mother-in-law asked him to build a dining table compatible with her Louis XVI chairs. Ruling out a contemporary piece, Newman thoroughly studied French historical furniture and developed an original table with accurate historical motifs. This reluctant entry into historical inspiration greatly affected Newman: "I felt sort of embarrassed about it. But when I started making it, I really enjoyed it because it was decorative and the forms were so much more interesting."[5] He began to realize the possible benefits of understanding and assimilating the volume, line, and surface of past work but interpreting it with personal elements and techniques. Newman's excitement in making the piece, and the response it received, were a revelation to him. The work neatly integrated his banjo-detailing and cabinetmaking skills.

Since 1981, Newman has continued to probe the fine points of neoclassical furniture and to develop his own rendition of the style. He uses ebony stringing, figured panels, and ornamental metal like a banjo-maker, and has also developed special tools, such as a spiral fluting jig, to explore new directions. Newman's fastidious attention to technical details and problem solving is legendary among furnituremakers. He himself admits, "I invariably get carried away with the construction of these things and do all sorts of things that are just so

Fig. b.   Blanket chest. Rochester, New York, 1980. Mahogany, cedar.
H: 20 in., W: 44 in., D: 20 in. Private collection.

much more time-consuming." As a result Newman and his one or two assistants focus more on quality and creativity than profit. His work has been featured in several shows at Gallery Henoch and Pritam & Eames.

Newman's recent commode (cat. 14) demonstrates his ability to adapt the ideas used in his classical tables to a monumental piece of case furniture.[6] The bold size, curved facade, and graceful combination of materials of Thomas Seymour's commode (fig. a) had intrigued Newman for several years; he viewed it as the quintessential example of the American Federal style. Newman changed the shape of the carcass from demi-lune to ellipse, even extending the curve past the 180-degree mark; he replaced the cockbeaded drawers with fielded-panel doors, preferring the look of large doors on the facade; and he altered the combination of woods from mahogany and bird's-eye maple to pearwood and curly maple. Newman relied on elaborate shaper jigs and cauls to make tight glue lines for the brick-laid doors and rails, top molding, and other necessary laminations. All the curly maple veneer is cut from a single board, and the pearwood boards were cut from the same tree and bookmatched to provide aesthetic symmetry. The commode thus demonstrates Newman's technical and aesthetic success in reinterpreting the past without slavishly copying it. He has improved the workmanship behind the form and reshaped it according to his own eye.

Fig. c.   Banjo. Rochester, New York, 1975. Curly maple, ebony; mother-of-pearl, brass, bronze. L: 36 in., W: 11 in., D: 2½ in. Private collection.

1.   Biographical information from Newman's response to author's questionnaire, June 1989; Ron Netsky, "Richard Newman," *Upstate Magazine* (January 8, 1984), pp. 7–12; Dick Lignum, "Interview: Richard Scott Newman," *The Workshop* 4 (spring 1984), pp. 10–11; conversations with the author, especially July 1988, and June 1989; and Newman's resume.

2.   Lignum, p.10.

3.   *Recent Art Furniture* (Niagara Falls, N.Y.: Niagara University, 1982), p. 31.

4.   Lignum, p. 10.

5.   Netsky, p. 9.

6.   Discussion of the piece is drawn from conversations with author, especially June 1989.

JERE OSGOOD

Fig. a. Desk and bookcase. Boston or Salem, Massachusetts, 1790-1800. Mahogany, white pine; mahogany veneer; glass; oil paint. H: 83½ in., W: 38 in., D: 24½ in. Museum of Fine Arts, Boston. The M. and M. Karolik Collection of 18th Century American Arts 1938.1829.

15 CYLINDER-FRONT DESK
Wilton, New Hampshire, 1989
Australian lacewood, Honduran rosewood, pearwood, mahogany plywood; Australian lacewood and pearwood veneers; Indonesian water buffalo calfskin
H: 45⅞ in., W: 43¼ in., D: 29 in.
Loaned by Jere Osgood

One of the fathers of the second generation of American studio furnituremakers, Jere Osgood (b. 1936) combines a profound interest in and knowledge of the intrinsic properties of wood with a compositional process that emphasizes extensive drawing and planning and a thorough exploration of appropriate techniques. His sensitivity to wood, economy of expression, and technical proficiency have enabled him to progress beyond the boxy designs and square joinery of his teacher Tage Frid to develop new designs that suggest natural wood forms and new techniques sympathetic to the material.

Osgood began making cabinets and repairing furniture when he was fourteen, working in his father's basement workshop.[1] His father taught him the proper use and care of tools and instilled an "if you need something, make it" philosophy. In 1955, Osgood enrolled at the University of Illinois, intending to become an architect like his grandfather. His architectural training provided him with a structured, methodical approach to visual problem solving. Yet, after two years, Osgood yearned for the more comfortable small environment of a furniture workshop and the ability to both visualize something and make it. He entered the School for American Craftsmen at the Rochester Institute of Technology (RIT) in the fall of 1959. Under Frid's tutelage, Osgood developed his technical skills and perfected his workmanship, but he felt constrained by his mentor's belief that technique determined design. Rather he firmly believed that one should design first, then figure out an appropriate technique.

After graduating from RIT with a B.F.A. in 1960, Osgood lived in Denmark for one year. Under the auspices of the Scandinavian Seminar, he familiarized himself with the refined, graceful furniture produced in small shops there, and augmented his technical repertoire. For example, recognizing the advantages of the horizontal mortiser, he made that part of his basic shop equipment. Upon his return to the States in 1961, Osgood lived for two years in Staten Island before moving to

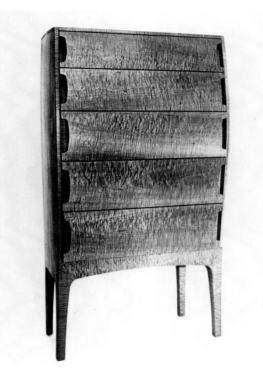

Fig. b. Chest of drawers. New Milford, Connecticut, 1969. Fiddleback Honduran mahogany. H: 59¾ in., W: 33 in., D: 17¼ in. Johnson Collection—Objects USA.

New Milford, Connecticut. Most of his work during the 1960s consisted of such accessories as trays, boxes, and small tables, which he sold predominantly through America House, the retail store of the American Craft Council. This work not only provided a steady income, allowing him to buy a truck, tools, and shop equipment, but also afforded him an opportunity to explore technical ideas on a discrete scale. Osgood also supplemented his income by teaching at the Craft Students League in New York City and the Brookfield Craft Center in Connecticut.

While establishing his shop, Osgood tried several experimental chairs, but it was not until the late 1960s that he really began to work in a larger scale. While drawing up new designs that would possess both strength and a sense of freedom, he began to explore new techniques to provide light structures with sensual three-dimensional shaping. Opposed to the heaviness and wasteful techniques of the stack lamination so popular in the late 1960s, Osgood developed a system of compound stave lamination: he sawed boards into thin strips and then glued them together in a mold to reprogram the wood into curves along two axes. He first used this technique on a 1969 chest of drawers for "Objects USA" (fig. b). The stave laminations of the side and the shaped compound laminations of the drawer fronts gave the chest a graceful bow. Laminating enabled him to build a stronger case with less waste and greater range of shapes than would have been possible by cutting from solid stock.[2]

Osgood used his lamination techniques to make the elliptical shell of a desk in 1970 (fig. c), and developed a new tapered bent lamination to create more natural, rootlike legs. Rather than simply trimming a bent laminated leg, exposing glue lines, and making a weaker lamination, Osgood developed a surface planer jig to make tapered strips that were then glued up in a tapered curve.[3] Osgood explained his preference for this technical solution to design: "I place more emphasis on pre-planning than shaping. The form comes from bending the wood into a light shell instead of removing stock. I'd rather spend my time drawing and drafting and making jigs than chopping away lumber. . . . I feel that lamination the way I use it follows the growth patterns in a tree better than can be achieved with traditional joinery techniques using square milled-to-thickness lumber."[4] Yet Osgood does make effective use of such techniques, an example being the false-cheeked tenoning on the front rails of his swelled chests of drawers.

Osgood's emphasis upon design and remarkable technical advances made him a desirable teacher in the 1970s. After replacing his friend Dan Jackson during Jackson's spring 1971 sabbatical from the Philadelphia College of Art, he was hired as assistant professor in woodworking and furniture design by Rochester Institute of Technology. He returned to New England in 1975 to accept a position at Boston University's Program in Artisanry, where he and Dan Jackson established the most dynamic furniture program of the late 1970s.

Although Osgood characteristically downplays his impact, referring to himself as "a working craftsman who just happens to teach," his activity in the 1970s dramatically shaped the course of the field. By teaching at three leading schools, he had the opportunity to reach a large number of students. His self-effacing disposition, open-minded approach to design solutions, and high expectations of compositional and technical work allowed him to affect a broad range of these students. Many have developed the skills and confidence necessary to pursue innovative directions.

Osgood ceased teaching in 1985, and he currently divides his time between speculative show work and commissions. His work in the 1970s and 1980s continued to explore and refine notions of natural swelling shapes achieved with appropriate and sympathetic woodworking techniques. The desk, in particular, has dominated his interests. Characteristic of his work of the mid-1980s is the desk in the 1986 "Craft Today" exhibition; double-bent tapered ash legs flow to form a central supporting pedestal for a slightly curved bubinga top with ash backboard.[5]

Fig. c.   Elliptical shell desk. New Milford, Connecticut, 1970. Walnut, figured maple, ash. H: 48 in., W: 48 in., D: 36 in. Private collection.

While much of Osgood's case furniture of the 1980s features curved rootlike legs, his 1989 cylinder-front desk (cat. 15) sits on four vertical legs.[6] Osgood drew inspiration from a cylinder-front desk and bookcase in the American furniture collection of the Museum of Fine Arts (fig. a). The quarter-round profile of the case and the mechanism that allows the movement of the covering lid—a method of concealment he first explored in 1970—intrigued him. To achieve a subtly organic appearance with rich figure, he selected Australian lacewood for its rich speckled surface, and used tapered bent laminations for the leg structure. The absence of noticeable lamination lines, the slight bends in the legs, and the rounded surfaces and softened edges make the legs flow naturally and gracefully from the miter joint at the top rear corner. The carcass of the desk also exhibits three-dimensional shaping—the lacewood sides and cylinder front are veneered over a plywood core that bulges slightly and dips below the horizontal rails.

The interior is more richly executed than those of Osgood's other desks. In addition to using a rich skin framed by rosewood, he devoted more attention to the pigeonholes and drawers. Drawing inspiration from eighteenth century desk interiors, he used shaped and tapered dividers of rosewood between the pigeonholes and rounded the underside of the rosewood drawer fronts. Dramatic contrasts in color—red calfskin, purplish rosewood, and pink pearwood—provide a sensual, rich composition, making the drawers and pigeonholes seem to float within the pearwood.

1.   Biographical information from Osgood's response to author's questionnaire, December 1988; his resume; conversations with the author, January and May 1989; Michael Stone, *Contemporary American Woodworkers* (Salt Lake City: Peregrine Smith, 1986), pp. 144–59; and Rosanne Somerson, "Perfect Sweep," *American Craft* 45, no. 3 (June/July 1985) pp. 30–34.

2.   For an explication of his technique, see Jere Osgood, "Bending Compound Curves," *Fine Woodworking* 17 (July/August 1979), pp. 57–60.

3.   Osgood wrote about this method in "Tapered Lamination," *Fine Woodworking* 14 (January/February 1979), pp. 48–51.

4.   Stone, p. 149.

5.   Paul Smith and Edward Lucie-Smith, *Craft Today: Poetry of the Physical* (New York: American Craft Museum, 1986), p. 149.

6.   The discussion of the desk is based on conversation with author, January and June 1989.

TIMOTHY PHILBRICK

16 DRESSING TABLE
Narragansett, Rhode Island, 1989
Ceylonese satinwood, Honduran mahogany; medium-density fiberboard; curly English sycamore veneer; yorkite; Macassar ebony, maple, and palmwood banding
H: 30 in., W: 36 in., D: 17 ⅜ in.
Loaned by Timothy Philbrick

Demonstrating the second generation's respect for historic furniture, Timothy Philbrick (b. 1952) recasts traditional eighteenth-century American furniture with a contemporary feeling. The quiet stylishness, gentle curves, subtle shaping, and innate sense of wood apparent in his work have earned the respect of his peers and encouraged many to probe historical prototypes.

As a youth, Philbrick derived considerable pleasure and satisfaction from working wood with hand tools.[1] He was especially drawn to the immediacy of the process, a feeling that was reinforced by a weekly ceramics class at the Rhode Island School of Design (RISD). His father, a Brown University professor and poet, recognized his son's fascination with woodworking and encouraged him to follow his interest rather than pursue a traditional career path. Consequently, upon his graduation from high school, Philbrick began an apprenticeship with John C. Northup, Jr., a cabinetmaker and restorer in North Kingston, Rhode Island. Philbrick learned a great deal about traditional techniques, and his exposure to a large number of historic antiques showed him what techniques worked and what lines pleased.

After four-and-a-half years, however, Philbrick felt himself confined by Northup's view, shared by many other makers of antique furniture, that no decent American furniture was made much after 1800. Philbrick believed that good work has been produced during every decade and that a furnituremaker should study design history to recognize this continuum. Unfortunately RISD lacked any design history classes at that time, so Philbrick turned for advice to John Kirk, a family acquaintance who had been curator at the Rhode Island Historical Society. Kirk had just accepted a teaching position at Boston University, and he encouraged Philbrick to apply to the newly established Program in Artisanry (PIA) there. PIA proved an ideal environment for Philbrick: he studied furniture history with Kirk; expanded his design and technical

Fig. a.   Dressing table. William Hook (1777-1867). Salem, Massachusetts, 1808-09. Mahogany, white pine; bird's-eye maple, satinwood, mahogany veneers. H: 30⅝ in., W: 35⅝ in., D: 19 in. Museum of Fine Arts, Boston. Gift of Mrs. John B.M. Mactaggart 39.556.

skills with Jere Osgood, Dan Jackson, and Alphonse Mattia; and focused exclusively on furniture as a candidate for a Certificate of Mastery. In return, Philbrick's amiable nature and fastidious workmanship made the subtle strengths of historic furniture—from Egyptian through the work of Emile Jacques Ruhlmann—more accessible to the other students, broadening their frame of reference.

Since graduating in 1978, Philbrick has run a very successful furniture shop. He works predominantly on commissions, but his work has been included in such prestigious galleries as Richard Kagan, Snyderman, Pritam & Eames, and Workbench. His work is also in the permanent collection of the Museum of Fine Arts, Boston, and the Rhode Island School of Design Museum of Art.[2]

While a student at PIA, Philbrick wrote a seminal article on proportions in eighteenth-century American furniture.[3] A concern with proportion remains at the heart of Philbrick's design; in his recent work, he continues to explore his concern with the relationship of parts that creates "graceful, balanced, and sensuous."[4] To complement this structural clarity, Philbrick carefully chooses grain patterns and colors to enhance the curves and shaping of his work. He draws from his experience at PIA, where Osgood taught him the use of bent laminations to build curved rails, and Jackson emphasized the impact of subtle shaping. In Philbrick's mature work, slightly bowed rails and delicately shaped and tapered legs convey a certain energy, and the familiar forms are given a more modern feeling (fig. b). Recently Philbrick has rediscovered turning, a skill he had acquired as an apprentice. He has successfully applied his own personal aesthetic and proportional system to lathe-turned legs to create dramatic movement on both the horizontal and vertical axes.

Inspired by the fine lines and proportions of the dressing table made by William Hook, in Salem in 1808 or 1809 (fig. a), Philbrick adapted its bowed front, canted corners, and the corner presentation of its front legs in his most recent table (cat. 16). He eliminated the carved molding around the top and the elaborate veneers on the front rail and concentrated his decoration on the top and the edge banding. Instead of using dark mahogany with lighter satinwood or flame birch veneers as Hook had done, Philbrick followed English fashion of the 1790s and used light satinwood with light curly sycamore. Philbrick further refined his design by gently blocking the

front rail to emphasize the grain of the tangential-cut satinwood, turning swelled capitals at the top of the legs to echo the blocked front, orienting the grain of the side rails to provide a lifting movement that complements the serpentine shape, and slightly bowing the rear rail. The subtle shaping of the elements; the pleasing relationship of parts; the restrained use of curly sycamore, ebony, and satinwood; and the palmwood, ebony, and maple edge banding make Philbrick's table a quiet but eloquent work.

Philbrick's soft-spoken, traditionally based work demands serious and sustained study. While his work has not attracted wide public acclaim, fellow furnituremakers and serious collectors recognize its sophistication and the important role he has played in developing the historical approach of second-generation furnituremakers.

1. Biographical information from Philbrick's response to author's questionnaire, January 1989; and from his resume.
2. On the RISD desk, see *Bulletin of Rhode Island School of Design: Museum Notes 1984*, 71, no. 2 (October 1984), p. 25.
3. "Tall Chests: The Art of Proportioning," *Fine Woodworking* 9 (winter 1977), pp. 39–43.
4. Quotation from "Portfolio: Timothy Philbrick," *American Craft* 46, no. 6 (December 1986/January 1987), pp. 56–57.

Fig. b.   Grecian sofa. Narragansett, Rhode Island, 1985. Curly maple;
silk cover and trimming. H: 32 in., L: 66 in., D: 24 in. Private collection.

MICHAEL PIERSCHALLA

17 TABLE

New Bedford, Massachusetts, 1989
Walnut, walnut burl, ebony, cherry; patinated copper;
ebonizing
H: 36 in., W: 20¼ in., D: 16½ in.
Loaned by Michael Pierschalla

In many ways, Michael Pierschalla (b. 1955) exemplifies the maturity of studio furnituremaking in the 1980s. At the beginning of the decade he was producing solid-wood, orderly, functional furniture as a student at the Rochester Institute of Technology (RIT). By the middle of the decade, he had increasingly used painted, textured surfaces to break up the slickness of his earlier work. Since joining the faculty in 1986 of the Program in Artisanry (PIA), currently within Southeastern Massachusetts University, Pierschalla has adopted a deconstructionist approach to furniture—taking apart, rearranging or reshaping parts to highlight its expressive aspects.

Pierschalla's introduction to woodworking was through his father, an inveterate craftsman who demonstrated the virtues of technical savvy and manual competence by fixing a variety of household goods, and recycling discarded materials.[1] Pierschalla's father encouraged his son to pick up some of these skills, but did not steer him into a career in wood.

During his freshman year at the University of Wisconsin, Pierschalla suddenly became deaf. Profoundly affected by the loss of his hearing, he withdrew to the familiar confines of his father's workshop and maintained some sense of usefulness and productivity by making things out of two-by-fours. Encouraged by a painter friend to develop a non-verbal language, Pierschalla took art courses and discovered a knack for visual thinking. He thought about art, read art history, and looked at paintings, but felt frustrated by the "uselessness" of flat, two-dimensional pictures. Instead he applied his new visual sensitivity to his basement woodworking. Intitially he felt as if he were the only person applying artistic principles and goals to a "manual trade."

His sense of isolation disappeared in 1977 when he discovered the writings of James Krenov. Krenov ennobled and intellectualized woodworking for Pierschalla, transforming it from a non-intellectual working-class pursuit into a dignified, soulful commitment. Krenov's books also helped Pierschalla realize the source of his attraction to wood—it required logical,

Fig. a.   Table. New Hampshire, 1740–60. Cherry, birch. H: 25⁵/₁₇ in.,
D: 26 in. Museum of Fine Arts, Boston. Gift of Hollis French 40.609.

Fig. b.   Writing desk. Smithville, Tennessee, 1983. Baltic birch plywood, English brown oak; English brown oak veneer; leather, Norcore; lacquer. H: 30 in., W: 60 in., D: 20 in. Private collection.

linear thinking; the final results embodied balance and usefulness; and the methodical processes demanded perfection. In short he realized that in making furniture, "I was really making myself over again."[2]

Resolved to pursue a furnituremaking career, Pierschalla rejected apprenticeship—he felt it anachronistic, and his familial values emphasized academic credentials—and enrolled at RIT. Before being allowed into the wood studio, however, Pierschalla had to spend a year at the National Technical Institute for the Deaf. While his one-year wait at NTID made him even more determined, Pierschalla found the environment at RIT in the late 1970s conservative and tradition-bound.[3] After two years Pierschalla transferred to the Appalachian Center for Crafts in Smithville, Tennessee, to work and study with Thomas Hucker and Wendy Maruyama. The open environment and ability to make and talk about furniture with sound construction and sufficient content provided Pierschalla with peace and purpose. Working with Maruyama from 1982 to 1983, he explored the use of surface texture and paint (fig.b) and began to show his work at the Workbench Gallery.

After spending two years at the Appalachian Center, Pierschalla set up a studio in the Emily Street shop in Cambridge. Sharing space with Judy Kensley McKie, Mitch Ryerson, Tom

Loeser, and others further encouraged him to continue his search for deeper content. He stopped relying so heavily on drawing and planning his decorative detailing, restricting such conventions primarily to form and construction. Instead he developed a freedom to sculpt directly with wood and use furniture as a means to examine sculptural concerns. He began to use wood, materials such as ColorCore, and paint to explore the idea of furniture as metaphor, as a vehicle to convey visual, intellectual, or emotional information. His work also gained greater visibility during this period: he made a pair of monumental tall-back chairs for "Material Evidence: New Color Techniques in Handmade Furniture" and a table for "Craft Today: Poetry of the Physical" at the American Craft Museum, and showed his work at Snyderman Gallery and the Society of Arts and Crafts.[4]

In late 1985 Pierschalla recovered most of his hearing and was overwhelmed by the cacophony of audio input. His former quiet continuum of thoughts gave way to a noisy fragmentation of information, ideas, and time. The speed and variety of this sensory explosion shaped his view of the world, and he began to see furniture forms in a fragmented fashion. Shortly thereafter he began to teach at PIA, which had been taken over by the Swain School of Design and subsequently by Southeastern Massachusetts University, and he developed his ideas. Although teaching drains time and energy, Pierschalla has continued to refine his ideas about pieces or fragments of furniture "dislocated and rediscovered in another context."[5]

In a series of small tables made in the last three years he has explored combinations of dissimilar parts and elements. Pierschalla's most recent table (cat. 17) represents his most ambitious and most sculptural effort in the table series. While derived very loosely from small cabriole-legged tables (fig. a), his table features a variety of details drawn from colonial American furniture and furnituremaking: two legs are roughed-out cabriole legs without any shaping; one leg resembles the template a cabinetmaker used as a pattern. The copper and ebony detailing on another leg was derived from the gilded molding of a looking glass; the patinated copper panel on the bent-laminated rail joined to the two cabriole legs features a cyma profile also found on chairs and tables of the eighteenth century. The patinated copper echoes the color of a painted seventeenth-century great chair in the Museum of Fine Arts. Pierschalla uses these elements within a new formal context to address spatial concerns. Distinguished from his earlier glass-topped tables by the variety of elements and his lack of interest in function, this table's only reference to function is its small patinated copper shelf. Pierschalla explains, "I am not especially interested in function anymore . . . I like furniture that works, I just think there are other things to do."[6] The copper shelf serves an important visual role: it provides additional circular motion to the canted ring running within the legs, and the slightly raised keystone element echoes the cross-section of the ebonized cherry leg. The compositional strength, the relationship of elements, and the allusion to function make Pierschalla's table a very sculptural piece of furniture.

1. Biographical information from Pierschalla's response to author's questionnaire, June 1989; conversation with the author, January 1989; and letter to the author, March 1989.

2. Questionnaire.

3. *Ibid.*

4. The chairs are illustrated in *Material Evidence: New Color Techniques in Handmade Furniture* (Washington, D.C.: Smithsonian Institution, 1985), p. 27; and the table is illustrated in Paul Smith and Edward Lucie-Smith, *Craft Today: Poetry of the Physical* (New York: American Craft Museum, 1986), p. 150.

5. Letter to the author, March 1989.

6. Questionnaire.

MITCH RYERSON

Fig. a.   Great chair. Boston, Massachusetts, 1665–80. Oak, maple; leather, brass nails. H: 38 in., W: 23⅝ in., D: 16⅜ in. Museum of Fine Arts, Boston. Seth K. Sweetser Fund 1977.711.

18 BENCH
Cambridge, Massachusetts, 1989
Cherry, Baltic birch plywood, veneer-core maple; mohair, silk cord, rayon tassels; oil paint
H: 49¼ in., W: 66½ in., D: 18½ in.
Loaned by Mitch Ryerson

For Mitch Ryerson (b. 1955), furniture reflects the lives and personalities of both maker and user. He is drawn to the effects of aging or use over time, the relationships of different surface treatments, the elements of massing, the subtleties of narrative, and the joy of whimsy. Within the parameters of function, Ryerson makes furniture with an irresistible personality that invites engagement and enjoyment.

As a boy, Ryerson found the hands-on emphasis of woodworking very exciting and satisfying. His interest in integrating physical and cerebral exercise drew him to wood, specifically wooden boats.[1] For one-and-a-half years, he studied boat building at the Washington County Vocational Technical Institute in Lubec, Maine, one of the few training programs in traditional boat building that existed in 1973. The intricate joinery and concern for wood movement of boat-building gave him a more sophisticated, three-dimensional approach to wood than the rough techniques and two-dimensional geometry of frame carpentry. Exposure to Maine boat builders also profoundly shaped Ryerson's attitudes—he recognized the importance of working directly and simply without becoming overly self-absorbed.

Between 1974 and 1978, Ryerson worked in boat shops, first in Brooklin, Maine, and then in Boston. While working in the cooperative Waterfront Workshop in Boston, he repaired and built work boats, fitted boat interiors, and even tried his hand at furniture design and construction. The attraction of the last led him to take a summer course at Boston University's Program in Artisanry (PIA). Exhilarated by the experience and his friendship with such PIA students as John Everdell, Ryerson enrolled at PIA in 1978. Initially Ryerson applied many of his boat-building techniques to furniture—especially steam bending wood and riveting—but by his graduation in 1982 he had begun to use more geometric lines and shapes to suggest personality in his furniture. He often used chair backs to present profiles of people's faces. This earlier work was featured in such prominent galleries as Workbench, Pritam

Fig. b. *Menage A Trois*. Cambridge, Massachusetts, 1985. Maple, plywood; oil paint. H: 44 in., W: 45 in., D: 21 in. Private collection.

Fig. c. Children's rockers. Cambridge, Massachusetts, 1986. Maple, cherry; clothespins, washboards, laundry detergent labels; oil paint. H: 26 in., W: 12 in., D: 21 in. Private collections.

& Eames, and Snyderman, as well as the Victoria and Albert Museum.

In 1984, Ryerson began to use vibrant color to delineate his severe shapes. Strong, contrasting colors emphasized the distinctions between the parts of his work and provided another level for viewer or user interaction (fig. b).[2] At the same time, he incorporated such everyday objects as scrub boards and fruit crate labels to trigger recognition and create new associations. His ideas for the children's rockers (fig. c), for example, sprang from the most concrete aspect of child-rearing, the mounds of laundry that overwhelmed Ryerson the new father.

More recently Ryerson has combined his narrative and geometric interests and produced a body of new work characterized by a freer, less overworked composition. Much of Ryerson's maturation can be attributed to his interest in the subtleties of traditional Native American or Appalachian craftsmen and to the supportive environment of the Emily Street cooperative in Cambridge, Massachusetts. Working in a building with such furnituremakers as Everdell, Judy Kensley McKie, and Tom Loeser has enabled him to benefit from the cooperative interchange between peers while pursuing his own vision. He recently summed up his mature view as follows: "I use color, playful arrangement, historical references, and anything else I can think of to make furniture that I hope is irresistibly inviting and reasonably functional."[3]

Ryerson's *Elizabethan Cabinet* (fig. d), combines the geometry of a sectional cornice and base molding, the aged effect of rubbed paint, and the figural emphasis of a carved door panel to produce a very strong piece of work. The powerful expression of the soulful medieval or playing card character, the interplay between worn paint and subtle solid colors, and visual movement of the ribbed moldings and the different shaping-coloring patterns of the door give the cabinet considerable depth and variety.

A merging of geometry and figure can also be seen on Ryerson's bench (cat. 18). Intrigued by the symbolic patriarchal connotations of a "great chair" (fig. a), the contrast of the dark severe structure and the soft squab, and the vitality of the ball turnings of the front stretcher, he developed a new design that inverts the qualities of the inspirational chair. Instead of replicating an intimidating, high-seated, magisterial dark throne vested with a single authority, Ryserson made a more

inviting, lower-seated, playfully colored bench for three. Rather than covering the parts of the frame with dark stain or leather, he painted the different parts with vivid contrasting colors, all of which are separated by refined edge lines of different hue. He even inverted the turned-ball motif of the great chair's front stretcher, sawing it out in inverse on the back panels of the bench. The twist of the traditional elements, the playfully painted and tasseled decoration, and the tension between formality and informality give the bench an air of hip familiarity and force the viewer to pause and think.

1. Biographical information from Ryerson's response to author's questionnaire, January 1989; his resume; and conversation with the author, April 1989.
2. For a discussion of such work, see Roger Holmes, "Color and Wood," *Fine Woodworking* 41 (July/August 1983), pp. 70–73.
3. *American Craft* 46, no. 3 (June/July 1986), pp. 48–49.

Fig. d.   *Elizabethan Cabinet.* Cambridge, Massachusetts, 1988. Mahogany, maple, basswood, Baltic birch plywood, aromatic cedar; oil paint, milk paint. H: 78 in., W: 26 in., D: 13 in. Museum of Fine Arts, Boston. Gift of Anne and Ronald Abramson 1988.337.

PAUL SASSO

19 *NO, YOU GET OUT OF MY GARDEN*
Almo, Kentucky, 1989
Bent laminated Lauan plywood, yellow poplar, curly maple,
wenge; curly maple and wenge veneers; acrylic paint, Rohplex
H: 30¼ in., W: 23½ in., D: 19½ in.
Loaned by Paul Sasso

While Paul Sasso (b. 1948) refers to his own "seat of the
pants" workmanship and credits his final forms to "sculpture
fairy visitation," his furniture is a calculated mix of engineering and intuition. He uses his carpentry and woodworking
experience and his training in art to give three-dimensional
form to his ideas about our culture.[1]

Sasso maintains that "making things is in my bones." As a
youth in Ontario he played in piles of salvage or left-over wood
collected by his father, who was in the construction business.
Wood was easily sawn and nailed, so Sasso made freewheeling
forts and airplanes that allowed him to have fun in his own
fantasy world.

After high school, Sasso worked for four years in the automobile industry. However, the tedium of assembly-line work,
his visual interests, and the opening of Canadian universities
to adult students in 1970 prompted him to study sculpture. At
the University of Windsor in Ontario, a sculpture professor
named William C. Law encouraged Sasso's interest in making
things. At first he worked in metal and plastic, but soon became
bored and impatient with the secondary processes involved
with these media. He returned to wood for its directness and
familiarity, using only a bandsaw and hand tools. Carpentry
and cabinetmaking jobs supported him through college. Lacking formal woodworking education, Sasso taught himself
through experimentation, and read everything he could on
joinery and wood technology.

After graduating from Windsor in 1978, Sasso earned an
M.F.A. in sculpture in 1981 from the University of Tennessee.
One of his professors there, F. Clark Stewart, encouraged
Sasso to apply the acrylic painting techniques he had learned
from Whitney Leland to his own wooden sculpture (fig. b). In
1981, Sasso merged his talents in woodworking and painted
sculpture to produce distinctive carved and painted furniture.
In the same year, he began to teach at Murray State University
in Kentucky, transforming the design and materials course into
one on functional design. This change in curriculum allowed

Fig. a.   Game and work table. Boston, Massachusetts, 1820-30. Mahog-
any, birch, rosewood. H: 30 in. W (leaves extended): 40¼ in., D: 17 in.
Museum of Fine Arts, Boston. Gift of William N. Banks and Frank Bemis
Fund 1976.621.

him to explore intellectually and technically his new path.

Sasso continues to teach at Murray State while producing about five pieces of furniture a year. His work of the late 1980s is thoughtful and immediate. He attributes his distinctive, vivid glazed colors and his rich patterning of hard-edge cartoon-style forms to the influence of "Big Daddy" Ed Roth, a California custom car maker in the 1960s. Sasso relies on carving and shaping to provide warmth and to articulate concept. Consistent features of his work include cabriole legs, inviting and elegant shapes, and beaded lines between forms or planes that serve as line drawings in real space.

Sasso's recent work demonstrates his growing technical sophistication. Bent laminations, panel construction, and a

Fig. b. *Baloney & Child Enthroned—Bad Baloney #3.* Knoxville, Tennessee, 1980. Mahogany, poplar; acrylic paint. H: 14 in., W: 16 in., D: 5 in. Private collection.

variety of strong and stable joints maximize strength and minimize wood movement, important issues for painted furniture. He also works efficiently with his material. For added carving bulk, he will epoxy on a preshaped piece or series of small preshaped blocks to provide more accurate visualization of the final shape and to avoid "wasting away" too much wood. He roughs out his carving with air-powered disc grinders and then refines his work with gouges, chisels, and a knife.

In spite of his technical repertoire, however, Sasso does not compromise the content of his furniture for its craftsmanship. His playful imagery often disguises ironic or cynical themes. Drawing upon the viewpoint of the artist Marcel Duchamp and the writings of the anthropologist Edmund Carpenter, Sasso treats his furniture as a form of social commentary, exploring class distinctions, rituals, and gender roles.

Gender is at the heart of *No, You Get Out of My Garden* (cat. 19).[2] The early nineteenth-century work and gaming table from which he drew inspiration (fig. a) attracted him both for its complex form and cultural significance. Work tables, with suspended fabric bags or wooden compartments in which a gentle lady could keep her needlework projects, were an important gender-specific artifact in the early nineteenth century. They embodied and reflected the new domestic sphere to which upper-class women were restricted.[3]

From the basic shape, Sasso began to focus upon issues of femininity. Interpreting the carcass shape as the *mons veneris*, he transformed the original's base carving into a richly massed skirt. Along the top edge, he carved and painted fixed leaves to carry through the textile imagery, eschewing the hinged functional leaves of the prototype. The yoke-shaped support structure of the inspirational table, which had allowed the half-drum shaped work compartment to slide in and out, was unnecessary in Sasso's drawered carcass. Nevertheless he used the idea of this strut to decorate the sides: he epoxied a strip of yellow poplar into a routed groove in the side and then shaped it to blend into the carcass. To further emphasize the theme of femininity he made his drawers "fancy." They feature curly maple bottoms with wenge bordering, and wenge sides with maple tops. The lowest drawer has rounded sides leading to a thin flat wenge bottom.

Sasso did not decide upon a palette or design for his painted surface until the form was finished.[4] Exploring his various memories and images of women, he remembered the woman who ran a corner variety store in Knoxville; her pink floral-patterned dress provided the inspiration for the overall decoration. Randomly scattered eliptical motifs represent vaginal lips. He built these up by cutting out masking tape with pinking shears, which he associated with women's fabric work, and then applying paint within the boundary of the tape.

Sasso's inspiration for the inner surface of the hinged top was the naive sophistication of landscape painting on early nineteenth-century painted furniture. His interest in landscape led him to visualize Mother Earth, represented by mountains and reinforced by the colorful skirt along the right edge. Above the landscape, he painted the patriarchal finger of God coming out of the sky, an image that appeared vividly in a dream of his. To Sasso, the finger represents the controlling tendency of males. To symbolize his own rejection of this sexist patriarchal system, he painted a pair of scissors piercing the finger, a traditional female instrument used in a violent male manner. The title reinforces this notion of women's self-assertion and self-definition.

No, You Get Out of My Garden thus demonstrates Sasso's adroit merging of playful, humorous decoration with sharp, analytical composition to make visually enjoyable but intellectually provocative furniture with a "presence that is not so loud . . . kinda comforting, and with its own intelligence."

1. Biographical information from Sasso's responses to author's questionnaire, December 1988; and conversations with the author, especially May 1987 and May 1989.
2. The discussion of *No, You Get Out of My Garden* is based upon the journal Sasso kept while working on the sewing table.
3. On the rise of the domestic sphere, see Nancy Cott, *The Bonds of Womanhood* (New Haven: Yale University Press, 1977).
4. The exegesis of the decoration is based on a conversation with the author, May 1989.

JAMES SCHRIBER

New Milford, Connecticut, 1989
Maple, cherry, birch plywood; bird's-eye maple veneer;
aluminum, industrial casters; milk paint
H: 51¼ in., W: 44 in., D: 19 in.
Loaned by James Schriber

James Schriber (b. 1952) incorporates painted surfaces and
architectural compositions to produce strongly designed traditional forms with contemporary references and details. His
work is firmly based on historical furniture—from seventeenth-century joined furniture to Shaker stands to furniture
designed by Frank Lloyd Wright—but he has recast it within
very modern parameters. He explains, "I felt free to borrow
elements and motifs from a variety of unrelated sources (or
related if you share my viewpoint). Where I could not borrow,
I guess I had to invent. I think the process is called designing."[1]

   Schriber majored in architecture at Goddard College,
whose holistic approach combined designing and hands-on
building.[2] Schriber's main instructor, David Sellers, sharpened
his visual sophistication and encouraged him not to neglect the
execution of a design. On Sellers's recommendation, in 1972
Schriber began to work with Randy Taplin, a local furnituremaker who worked in the straightforward manner of the first
generation studio woodworker: solid-wood construction, some
exposed joinery, natural finish, and a combination 1950s Dan-
ish-Shaker-Hippie style. Attracted by the scale of furniture
projects and the possibility of controlling a project from start
to finish, Schriber in 1973 set up shop with another Goddard
friend in the New Hamburger Commune in Plainfield, Vermont, and began to make relatively simple wood furniture.

   By 1974 many of Schriber's peers had moved on to architecture school or more defined areas, and Schriber himself
began to look for ways to advance his knowledge of furnituremaking. On a visit to Rochester, Schriber was both turned off
by the factory-like orientation and dull work at the Rochester
Institute of Technology, and overwhelmed by the energy and
work of Wendell Castle. Castle and Jere Osgood suggested
that the loose environment and intense instruction of Dan
Jackson at the Philadelphia College of Art (PCA) would be
inspirational. Schriber enrolled there in the fall of 1974 and,
under Jackson's guidance, he learned a great deal about furniture, joinery techniques, carving and shaping, and commit-

Fig. a.   Cupboard. New Hampshire, probably Hampton, 1700–40. White
pine, maple; oil paint. H: 49 in., W: 40½ in., D: 18¼ in. Museum of Fine
Arts, Boston. Bequest of Charles Hitchcock Tyler 32.250.

ment. Schriber followed his teacher in 1975 to the Program in Artisanry (PIA) at Boston University, where he received a Certificate of Mastery in 1979. John Kirk's emphasis on line and volume in historical furniture complemented Schriber's architectural design, Jere Osgood's instruction in lamination and structural simplicity augmented his technical repertoire, and Alphonse Mattia's sculptural humor balanced his serious designs.

While Schriber had deliberately focused on technical issues and labor-intensive decoration at PIA, after graduation he pragmatically altered his philosophy. Unable to earn a living making only custom furniture, he established a cabinet and architectural woodwork business specializing in sophisticated but easily made cabinets and furniture for New York City office and apartment buildings—"the biggest bang for the buck."[3]

This architectural work constitutes about one half of Schriber's activity, and its success has enabled him to hire three assistants, to buy equipment for his shop, and to continue making some exhibition work. His custom work, some of which is traditional (fig. b) and some of which is more architectural with a contemporary look (fig. c), has been shown at such galleries as Kagan, Snyderman, Pritam & Eames, and

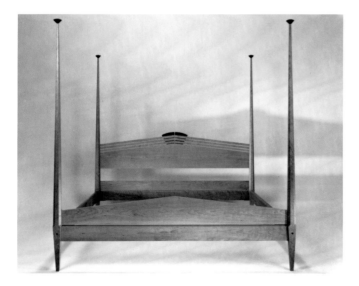

Fig. b.   Pencil post bed. New Milford, Connecticut, 1989. Cherry, macassar ebony. H: 88 in., W: 78 in., L: 80 in. Private collection.

Workbench, and in such important museum exhibitions as "Material Evidence: New Color Techniques in Handmade Furniture" and "Craft Today: Poetry of the Physical." Schriber has also organized exhibitions at the Brookfield Craft Center in Connecticut: the 1982 "Color/Wood" explored the various uses of color and paint in contemporary furniture, and the 1984 "Inspired by Folk Traditions" placed contemporary work within an aesthetic continuum. To provide an edge to his work and keep up with current trends in the visual arts, Schriber reads extensively—books and magazines on historical furniture, art journals, industrial design publications, and even automotive and rock-and-roll magazines.

For the current exhibition, Schriber responded to a painted, vernacular cupboard made in New Hampshire in the first half of the eighteenth century (fig. a). The historical piece appealed to him because it possessed a building-like mass and painted decoration. Its combination of elegant lines and less-serious detailing parallels much of Schriber's work. In place of the cabinetmaker's refined joinery, the rough, nailed carpenter's construction and the reliance on paint to disguise and unify also intrigued Schriber. He most enjoys work that is least labor intensive in construction and finish, enabling him to sustain the excitement of the original idea through execution, adjustment, and finish. Schriber articulates his philosophy clearly, "Painting frees you up, you don't have to worry about joinery, matching grain, what width the boards are. You can come up with any kind of form, and not have to rely on the same old shapes. We woodworkers end up worrying about things too much, overworking things to death. With painted stuff I know if I mess it up, I can put a little putty in it. It's fun. You can make something quick and enjoy working in the shop."[4]

Schriber found the single-door access in the upper section of the historical piece very limiting. To create more effective storage areas, he provided side doors for small compartments and used sliding circular doors for the center section (cat. 20). The latter provides not only easy access but a visual center and a technical surprise. In the spirit of the original piece, Schriber made laminated doors that slide in routed grooves rather than more sophisticated tambour doors. Uncomfortable with the looseness of the original's painted circular decoration, Schriber favored a smaller, more controlled form of patterning, relying on the geometry of the diamond panels behind the pulls, the quarter-round panels in the corners, and the kerf lines radiat-

Fig. c. Bedroom dressing unit. New Milford, Connecticut, 1989. Bird's-eye maple, birch plywood, holly, medium-density fiberboard; bird's-eye maple veneer; Avonite, nickel-plated perforated steel, nickel-plated brass, bone. H: 84 in., W: 108 in., D: 24 in. Private collection.

porary references or parts, and his own interest in combining wood and paint.

1. Letter to the author, June 24, 1988.
2. Biographical information from Schriber's response to author's questionnaire, May 1989; his resume; and conversations with the author, November 1987 and May 1989.
3. Questionnaire.
4. Schriber quoted in Roger Holmes, "Color and Wood," *Fine Woodworking* 41 (July/August 1983), p. 73.

ing from the pulls. He borrowed this idea of small patterning from Viennese designs from the early twentieth century.

Schriber's effective use of contemporary industrial accents is evident in his use of aluminum pulls and his choice of casters for the front feet. Searching for a quick way to make a ball foot, Schriber noticed that many seventeenth- and eighteenth-century nailed chests and cupboards had ball feet and brackets that were to be viewed from the side as two-dimensional profiles. Schriber takes a novel, contemporary approach to reinterpreting the tradition profile, using a "bootjack" profile for the rear foot and casters for the front.

In the New Hampshire piece, the maker used an opaque, overall paint, probably to hide the quick construction, to articulate the moldings and turnings, and to unify the composition. Schriber, on the other hand, used a thinner milk paint in combination with natural cherry and bird's-eye maple. He uses the paint not so much to disguise as to enrich aesthetic content, and consciously contrasts the two woods for similar effect.

Schriber successfully reworks a vernacular storage form and updates it with other historically derived ideas, contem-

TOMMY SIMPSON

21 *BOSTON THRONE CHAIR*
Washington, Connecticut, 1989
Walnut, cherry, padouk, mahogany, bird's-eye maple, spalted
maple, curly maple, tulip, yellow satinwood; bone, shell
H: 50 in., W: 32⅜ in., D: 24¾ in.
Loaned by Tommy Simpson

For Tommy Simpson (b. 1939) the utility or function of furniture has always been compatible with and enhanced by fantastic forms, natural motifs, *trompe l'oeil* details, and personal imagery. In contrast to the sophisticated but impersonal furniture of most post-World War II industrial design, Simpson's fanciful, whimsical furniture provides warmth and encourages reflection. Simpson uses verbal and visual puns and satire to probe the deeper meanings of cultural icons, American society, and memory. In the belief that "art can be meaningful and still give joy," Simpson uses humor to engage the eye and the mind.[1]

Trained in painting rather than in furniture design and construction, Simpson relies on his own intuitive sense of material and a painterly sense of composition.[2] As a child, he

Fig. a.   Windsor armchair. New England, 1760–90. Maple, white pine,
ash. H: 42¼ in., W: 18⅝ in., D: 21 in. Museum of Fine Arts, Boston.
Anonymous Gift 31.393.

enjoyed combining scrap wood and found materials. Encouraged by his great aunt, who taught him to paint, Simpson went on to study painting at Northern Illinois University. A course in printmaking from Keefe Baker taught Simpson to look beneath the surface composition to find a series of interlocking layers of meaning and intellectual content of the final work. This formal training allowed Simpson to explore the tension between individual formal elements and composition as a whole. The parts possessed their own identity or meaning, which could enhance or contradict the overall message.

While earning an M.F.A. in painting from the Cranbrook Academy of Art in 1964, Simpson began to focus upon furniture, both as a subject matter and as a three-dimensional canvas. Unfettered by traditional notions of cabinetmaking, he produced organically shaped forms with brightly polychromed abstract or comic-striplike surface decoration (fig. b). His pine carcasses were simply glued and pegged together with dowels. After shaping the elements, he applied an overall coat of gesso to provide a smooth ground and then painted the entire surface, usually with acrylics. Oftentimes he would use a gouge after the gesso or paint layers to provide additional shape and texture.[3]

Simpson's bright colors and sensual imagery brought him notoriety in Chicago and New York. One-man shows at J. Walter Thompson Co.'s World Gallery and P.V.I. Gallery attracted the attention of Paul Smith of the Museum of Contemporary Crafts, who recognized that Simpson was pursuing a path in furniture not unlike that of Peter Voulkos in ceramics. Due to Smith's interest, Simpson exhibited work in a number of the mid-1960s progressive craft art shows at the museum: "Amusements Is," "The Bed," and "Fantasy Furniture."

Simpson continued to produce his brightly painted sculptural work for gallery shows through the end of the 1960s, but by the early 1970s, he turned his energies to commissions, small gouache paintings, and teaching, which ultimately did not suit him. In the early 1970s he applied his humor and woodworking skills to making toy-like objects.[4]

In the mid 1970s, Simpson began to concentrate more on sculptural narrative pieces, somewhat like those of H.C. Westermann, but with an ironic humor rather than dark sarcasm (fig. c). The use of different woods, buttons, punched tin, and other found objects instead of paint was an important step for Simpson, and it made the meanings of his objects both more

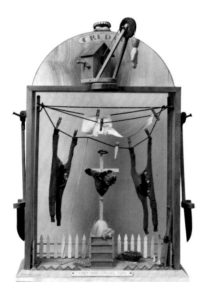

Fig. b. *Daphne Bed*. Elgin, Illinois, 1968. Pine; acrylic paint. H: 84 in., W: 48 in., L: 84 in. Private collection.

Fig. c. *Knit one—pearl two (crucifixion of a mitten)*. Greenwich, Connecticut, 1976. Mixed-media glass box construction. H: 40 in., W: 20 in., D: 8 in. Collection of Alan Brown.

accessible to the casual viewer and more provocative to the engaged viewer. He began to show these works in such galleries as Theo Portnoy and Fairtree.[5]

Beginning in about 1978, Simpson became interested in historical allusions and surreal juxtapositions of loaded images.[6] His new use of traditional ideas and techniques to make social commentary is clearly seen in his 1981 installation at the American Craft Museum (fig. d). By adapting historical painting techniques (stencilling, sponging, graining, and smoke-graining), historical conventions (landscapes and proscriptive sayings), and historical forms (lolling chairs and Windsor settees), Simpson created an updated notion of a colonial parlor. The environment graphically spoofs historical associations, popular sentimental taste, and even the art and technique of woodworking itself.[7]

Simpson's work in the 1980s continues to push and explore notions of memory and history. To provide color, he uses different types of woods and, in a few specific isolated areas, traditional graining or staining techniques. His workmanship has become more sophisticated since the 1960s, but he consciously makes his pieces unrefined. As he explains, "To make them spontaneous and straightforward makes them more childlike—they fit my theme of approachability better. A focus on too much craftsmanship seems too educated, too stiff, too dead."[8] Simpson has not rejected sound woodworking skills, he has merely emphasized tool marks and simple joinery rather than 440-grit sandpaper and complex joinery for their own sake.

Simpson's *Boston Throne Chair* (cat. 21) venerates the institution that organized the exhibition for which the chair was made. He has taken the Windsor armchair (fig. a)—a popular form in the early national period that has come to be associated with the country's founding fathers—but hyperbolized it by making the seat out of walnut, the legs out of purpleheart, and other parts out of exotic or figured woods. By painting with varieties of fine and exotic woods, rather than painting over common woods as traditional Windsor chairmakers did, Simpson gives the utilitarian form a symbolic presence. The throne also differs from typical Windsors in its lack of bilateral symmetry, instead drawing compositional energy from the incorporation of diverse decorative elements, each of which has been inspired by a piece of art in the Museum's permanent collection but executed in a more fanciful manner. The carved alligator of the medial stretcher is derived from an applied alligator mount on the cornice of an English wall cabinet made in about 1810; the shape of the front legs from the legs of a lady's desk made by Charles Beaudoine in New York during the 1850s; the reeding on the tops of the legs from the reeded legs of eastern Massachusetts Federal-period furniture. The shaped horn of the seat derives from the moonlit-water reflection in Edvard Munch's *Summer Night's Dream (The Voice)* of 1893, and the inlaid shell in the raised horn of the seat from the shell painted by John Rito Penniman on a semi-circular commode made by Thomas Seymour in 1809. The dedication date of the Museum's present building, 1909, is carved in a style similar to that on early eighteenth-century chests from Hadley, Massachusetts. The inlaid feathers in the middle of the seat come from a set of oval-back chairs with painted feathers made in Philadelphia in the late eighteenth century, and the scroll of the right arm and the carved purpleheart tassle underneath from Paul Cézanne's *Madame Cezanne in a Red Armchair* of 1877. Turned incisions on the tulip spindle behind the tassel are borrowed from the Japanese Edo period screen *Arrival of a Portuguese Ship in Japan*, and the panel of George Washington from the famous Gilbert Stuart portrait. The inlaid bone teapots on the back of the crest rail's ears recall John Copley's 1765 portrait of Paul Revere. The central finial is based on the finials of eighteenth-century New England high chests and chest-on-chests; and the carved birds flanking the finial allude to Paul Gaugin's painting *D'ou venons-nous? Que sommes-nous? Ou allons-nous? (Where Do We Come From? What Are We? Where Are We Going?)* of 1897. The Gaugin painting also provided Simpson with the idea for the carved maxim on the seat, "*Ou Sommes-Nous Assis. Ou Asseyons-Nous. Ou Assierons-Nous*" (*Where Did We Sit? Where Are We Sitting? Where Will We Sit?*). The philosophical origins of Simpson's questions provide yet another layer of symbolic humor to the throne.

Boston Throne clearly illustrates Simpson's interest in iconoclastic commentary of American culture, whimsically poking fun at art and art institutions, but using humor to inspire thoughtfulness. By playing on images, words, and associations, he has produced work that is both friendly and long-lasting.

Fig. d. *American Room* (detail). Installation at the American Craft Museum, New York City, 1981. Mixed media; paint. H: 8½ ft., W: 13 ft., D: 18 ft.

1. *Perspectives: Tommy Simpson* (Sheboygan, Wisc.: John Michael Kohler Arts Center, 1982), p. 2.

2. Information on Simpson's education is drawn from an interview with the author, April 1989.

3. Simpson's techniques and the range of his work are shown in Thomas Simpson, *Fantasy Furniture* (New York: Reinhold, 1968).

4. Letters from Simpson to furnituremaker Wendell Castle, 1971 and 1973. Archives of American Art, Wendell Castle Papers, undated correspondence, Box 1.

5. For the best discussion of this portion of Simpson's work, see Marshall Davidson, "Wooden Wiles of Tommy Simpson," *Craft Horizons* 38, no. 1 (February 1978), pp. 26–27.

6. *Perspectives*, p.2.

7. The installation is discussed in "Whimsy in Wood," *American Craft* 41, no. 6 (December 1981/January 1982), pp. 26–27.

8. Conversation with the author, June 1989.

ROSANNE SOMERSON

22 *BLACK LACE TABLE*
Westport, Massachusetts, 1989
Bird's-eye maple, maple; black lace slate, copper leaf; milk
paint, copper enamel paint
H: 16½ in., W: 41 in., D: 41 in.
Loaned by Rosanne Somerson

Rosanne Somerson (b. 1954) builds graceful forms with traditional materials, layers of detail, and delightful decoration
to entice the user or viewer to react, think, or imagine. Concerned with function, however loosely defined, and longevity,
she makes furniture that constantly encourages "a discovery
process, possibly through visual connections, alignments,
misalignments or combinations of materials, sometimes with
surprises in function or secrets."[1] As a teacher at the Rhode
Island School of Design (RISD), she has also helped students
approach furniture with a similar depth.

Somerson intended to major in photography when she
enrolled at the RISD in 1972.[2] By the end of the first semester
she had begun to feel frustrated by the limitations of two-
dimensional work and the amount of time spent in a chemical-

Fig. a. Side table. Philadelphia, Pennsylvania, 1760–80. Mahogany, yellow poplar; marble. H: 28⅞ in., W: 45⅝ in., D: 21 in. Museum of Fine Arts,
Boston. The M. and M. Karolik Collection of 18th Century American Arts
41.588.

laden dark room. During RISD's Wintersession, a six-week
interim semester in which students are encouraged to explore
outside of their major field of study, Somerson tried woodworking. Her father had built and worked on the house in
which she grew up, and the familiar sounds and smells of
woodworking made her feel less overwhelmed by the college
environment. She found the material alluring, and the process
intriguing and challenging, and she became fascinated with
the integration of problem solving and aesthetics. Somerson
changed her major first to sculpture and then to industrial
design—there was no undergraduate woodworking or furniture major at that time—in order to focus upon furnituremaking. Because the requirements of her major did not allow
enough experience in furniture, she took a semester off to
attend Peters Valley Craftsman, a New Jersey craft program,
to concentrate on building decorative furniture.

By the time she graduated in 1976, Somerson had a solid
foundation in the technical aspects of furnituremaking, but
she had also developed a broader perspective. Aware of the
work being done in such media as glass and ceramics, she was
frustrated by the lack of experimentation and personal expression in most woodworking. To incorporate such ideas into her
work, she drew from Russian Constructivism, Egyptian material culture, Japanese architecture, Art Deco graphic design,
and primitive art. The latter was important to Somerson for
several reasons: the evident joy of and respect for the maker in
that society, the soulfulness of the work, and the broad definition of function to include spiritual or evocative meaning.
These considerations became the core of her philosophy as
she began to design for the contemporary world.

After graduation, Somerson wrote and edited for *Fine
Woodworking* and taught woodworking to a wide range of students, from elementary school children at the Edward Devo-
tion school in Brookline, Massachusetts, to adult students
at the Harvard University Center for Continuing Education.
While making a living in this manner, she continued to draw
to develop and clarify her ideas on furniture. In the spring of
1978 she briefly rented space at the Emily Street cooperative in
Cambridge, Massachusetts, and began to make some furniture
based upon her drawings from the previous few years. Her
work began to evolve into its present form in 1979, when
Somerson and her husband bought a house in Roslindale,
Massachusetts, and set up a shop in an old barn. The barn

was her first real studio, and she finally began to make a living making furniture.

In 1979 Somerson showed work at Richard Kagan Gallery in Philadelphia and the Danforth Museum in Framingham, Massachusetts. These shows gave Somerson the exposure she needed. A 1979 table in the 1981 "Woodforms" exhibition at the Brockton Art Museum demonstrates Somerson's early approach. *High-Heeled Coffee Table* (fig. b) was inspired by a piece of Egyptian jewelry and incorporated ideas from African baskets, Art Deco hardware, and high-heeled shoes.[3] The coffee table gained Somerson additional visibility and Workbench Gallery began to show her work in 1982. Much of her furniture from the early 1980s was big and technically impressive, intended "to convince myself that I really could make significant pieces."[4] Being self-conscious about her skills, she sought to prove to herself that she could handle complex design and technical issues that still expressed her basic aesthetic ideas.

After demonstrating her skill with larger forms, a confident Somerson turned to smaller and lighter forms in which she could use more playful and expressive detailing. During this period she began to explore the possibilities of painted surfaces and detail. Her increased visibility had brought her more commissions and invitations for other shows. While the former paid bills, the latter allowed her to develop new ideas without the constraints of the client or repeating commissions

Fig. c.   *Earring Cabinet*. Westport, Massachusetts, 1986. Maple, padouk; metallic powder, metallic thread, handmade paper, mirror glass; oil paint. H: 27 in., W: 22 in., D: 7 in. Private collection.

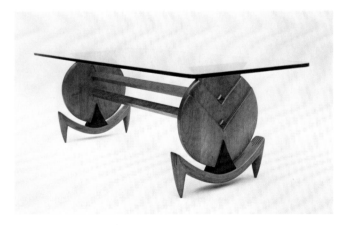

Fig. b.   *High-Heeled Coffee Table*. Roslindale, Massachusetts, 1979. Cherry, ebony; glass. H: 16¾ in., W: 50 in., D: 19 in. Private collection.

of old designs. Grants, such as the Visual Artists Fellowship that the National Endowment for the Arts awarded her in 1984, also provided money and blocks of time to explore new directions. Her interest in new directions was further stimulated in 1985 when she began to teach the graduate furniture program at RISD. Her earring cabinet of 1986 (fig. c) is the best example of her work from this period. Shaped like an earring, its function is self-evident, but Somerson endowed it with certain surprises and mysteries. The holding cup is merely a half-cup whose reflection in the mirror completes its form. The mirror also doubles the number of earrings stored in the cup. Somerson painted and glazed the frame of the mirror and the cabinet, building up a rich, fanciful surface. She lined the bottoms of the padouk drawers with handmade paper. The result is a delicate object that evokes an intimate response.

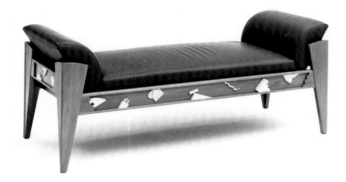

Fig. d.   Bench. Westport, Massachusetts, 1986. Pearwood, bleached soft curly maple; leather. H: 22¾ in., W: 57½ in., D: 22 ¼ in. Museum of Fine Arts, Boston. Gift of Anne and Ronald Abramson 1987.40.

Within the past three years Somerson has also produced a series of benches, couches, and daybeds that possess a subtle formality with small-scale shaped details. Previously she had sketched many pieces with marquetry decoration, but had never actually used the pictorial technique. On her couches and daybeds (fig. d) she began to apply three-dimensional relief carving. She set small, cut-out and shaped "jewels" of quiet solid wood within a rail of rich solid wood that serves as a frame. She then covered the seat with deeply colored leather.

Somerson works equally effectively in traditional, natural-finish pieces and innovative painted forms. Her use of each allows her to build rich compositions. "I make furniture that fuses function with ornament. My goal is to create inanimate objects that work into an intimate realm with the viewer. I hope to draw the viewer in first with pleasing overall form and a hint of mystery that will then attract the viewer to a closer relationship with the piece. My intention is that once some-one is drawn in, there will be surprises to discover about the piece. . . . I try to succeed in holding interest by layering the work with levels of detail that cause the viewer's eye to explore components of the piece."[5] Her success in this has been recog-nized recently by the National Endowment for the Arts, which awarded her a second Visual Artist Fellowship in 1988.

Black Lace Table (cat. 22) features legs similar to those of the benches and couches, but has a richer combination of materials—slate, copper leaf, and painted decoration. Drawing ideas from swell-skirted, stone-topped side tables of the past (fig. a), she altered the basic traditional materials slightly but respectfully to create a new table full of expressive elegance.[6] She updated the form, rejecting the frontal formality of a table that was intended to be placed against the wall and designing a form better suited to contemporary living: a less formal low table that would sit in the middle of a room and be seen from many different angles and heights. She constructed the frame of highly figured bird's-eye maple, used copper leaf to accen-tuate the swell of the skirt, and replaced the marble top with slate. In Somerson's exquisite combination of media, the bird's-eye maple enriches the dazzling figure of the slate, the copper leaf and sponged enamel details of the skirt pick up the slate's ore tones, the muted milk paint contrasts with the fig-ured slate and maple, and the scratch-carved skirt echoes the texture of the slate top.

1.   "Rosanne Somerson: Furniture Maker," *Women Artists News* 12, nos. 4 and 5 (fall/winter 1987), p. 17.

2.   Biographical information from "Rosanne Somerson: Furniture Maker," pp. 16–18; Somerson's response to author's questionnaire, January 1989; Joy Cattanach Smith, "Furniture: A Sculptural Medium," *Art New England* 7, no. 1 (December–January 1985–86), pp. 4–5; her resume; and numerous conversations with the author.

3.   *Woodforms* (Brockton, Mass.; Brockton Art Museum, 1981), p. 21.

4.   Questionnaire.

5.   Rosanne Somerson, "Artist's Statement" (1989).

6.   "Rosanne Somerson: Furniture Maker," pp. 16–18.

7.   The discussion of the table is based on conversation with the author, May 1989.

WENDY STAYMAN

Haydenville, Massachusetts, 1989
Swiss pearwood, curly maple, holly, medium-density
fiberboard, Baltic birch plywood; Swiss pearwood and curly
maple veneers; brass, silver, gold
H: 42 in., W: 51¼ in., D: 21¼ in.
Loaned by Wendy Stayman

Wendy Stayman (b. 1946) successfully combines two comple-
mentary careers: furnituremaking and object conservation. A
passionate interest in material, process, and the manifestation
of the creative impulse unites Stayman's varied work. In both
her conservation lab and her furniture studio, she strives to
broaden her own sense of materials and her own technique.
Stayman feels that the creative aspects of making furniture
enhance her conservation capabilities by allowing her to
exclude her own personal vision and be in complete empathy
with the original maker. At the same time, examining and conserving works of art provides unlimited stimulation from the
enormous variety of materials, techniques, and processes. Further, it allows her to view her own work within a much broader
context.[1]

After Stayman earned a B.A. in art history from the
University of Pennsylvania in 1970, she continued to search
for a more creative application of her aesthetic interests. She
apprenticed to a cabinetmaker-furniture restorer for one year
before becoming a conservation fellow at the University
Museum, University of Pennsylvania. Subsequent training in
conservation—she received a Master of Art Conservation from
Queen's University, Ontario—and three years as assistant con-
servator at the University Museum in Philadelphia provided
her with considerable knowledge of and technical experience
with an exceptional collection of archeological and ethno-
graphic materials. The conservation of museum artifacts
provided her with historical understanding, intellectual
stimulation, emotional engagement, and manual application.

While conserving several life-size wooden sculptures by
William Rush for an exhibition at the Pennsylvania Academy
of the Fine Arts, Stayman became increasingly interested in
wood and sought to expand her knowledge in that medium. In
1980, she took a furnituremaking course with Leonard Hilgner
at the Philadelphia College of Art and a wood identification
workshop from Bruce Hoadley at the University of Massa-

Fig. a.   Chest with two drawers. Enfield, Connecticut, about 1710. Oak,
pine. H: 41½ in., W: 44⅞ in., D: 20½ in. Museum of Fine Arts, Boston.
Bequest of Charles Hitchcock Tyler 32.216.

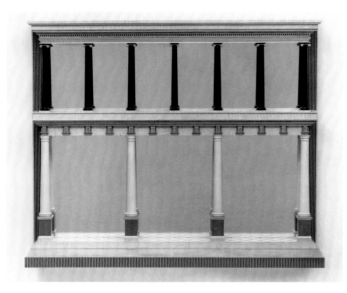

Fig. b. *Piazza del Solms* (Entryway Mirror). Easthampton, Massachusetts, 1986. Curly maple, maple, ebony, holly, cherry; ceramic capitals, stone; lacquer. H: 41½ in., W: 48 in., D: 12 in. Private collection.

chusetts, Amherst. In Hoadley's course she first heard of the Wendell Castle Workshop, a newly established program in furnituremaking and design. With funding provided by the Samuel H. Kress Foundation, Stayman took a one-year leave of absence to study furniture at the Castle school. This represented a pivotal point in her life—she was once again deeply involved with her own creative endeavors, but now realizing them in a different medium.

Stayman graduated from the two-year program at the Wendell Castle Workshop and continued there as an artist-in-residence for one more year. The stimulation and experimentation at the workshop enabled her to both master technique and explore her own creativity. Castle's own work was extremely diverse during these years, including stack lamination, *trompe l'oeil* narrative pieces, 1920s French revival, clocks, and painted sculptural furniture. Castle, Stephen Proctor (the dean of the workshop), and the other instructors emphasized design and idea, and taught a wide range of techniques to enact such ideas.

Based upon traditional forms and historical motifs, Stay-

man's work can be characterized as linear and architectural; she frequently uses light-colored woods and often includes accents of other materials to explore texture (fig. b), movement, controlled use of color, and a variety of decorative techniques. An avid collector of curious and exotic materials, she has amassed an impressive inventory for future work. Because her work is usually complex and labor intensive, Stayman often jobs-out technical aspects of her pieces to specialized craftsmen (fig. c).[2] This allows her to maintain an active production schedule and maximize her creative time.

Stayman's exhibition and commission schedules are busy. She feels that both approaches provide the opportunity to explore, get feedback, and gain insight and knowledge that provide additional growth. Speculation work often allows for a more open-ended exploration of new territory, while the often tighter parameters of commission work provide opportunity for re-exploration and refinement. Both are important—"You have to show your work if you have something to say. I try to keep my work out there."[3]

For "New American Furniture," Stayman responded to the aesthetic presence and historical association of a chest with two drawers from the Hadley area of Massachusetts in the Connecticut River Valley (fig. a). She was initially attracted to the bold straightforward shape, the surface decoration and texture, the proportions, and the obvious utilitarian nature of the chest. Her interests then extended to the tulip-and-leaf motif, the frequent inclusion of the owner's initials and a year on such chests, and the provenance near Stayman's Haydenville shop. Reinterpreting the form and decoration, she designed a very refined architectural case (cat. 23) instead of the joinerly, frame-and-panel look of the Hadley chest. For functional reasons, she eliminated the lift-top of the prototype, and, to increase storage space, she removed the rail between the two drawer fronts. In order not to obscure the strong linear form of the carcass and the handsome figure of the veneer, Stayman limited her carved decoration to the doors. Her chest retains the tulip-and-leaf motif and the sharp-edged relief of the historical version, but differs dramatically in appearance. Stayman conceived of the flowers and leaves as pictorial inlays into an all-over ribbed background. An Old Kingdom Egyptian limestone relief of *Ti Watching a Hippopotamus Hunt*, a favorite of Stayman's, suggested Stayman's integration of the historic tulip-and-leaf motif chest with

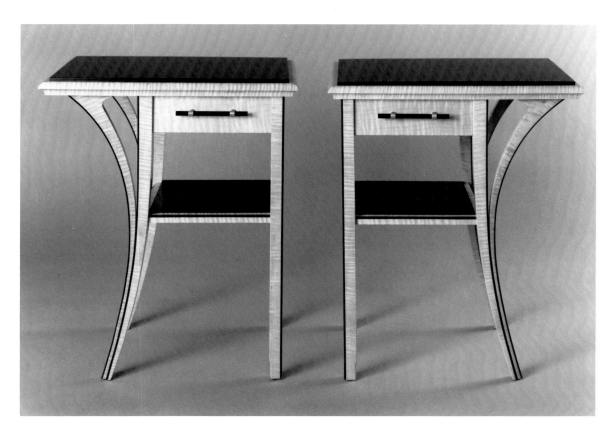

Fig. c.   End tables. Easthampton, Massachusetts, 1985. Curly maple, ebony; ebony veneer; brass. H: 24½ in., W: 20 in., D: 14 in. Private collection.

the ribbed background, a decorative detail she has explored extensively.[4]

In some of her early pieces, Stayman cut grooves into solid wood and lacquered the recesses (see fig. b). Later, she applied veneers over solid wood of a contrasting color, then cut back through the veneers to the solid, producing surface patterning. On her Haydenville chest, she has cut through the curly maple veneer to expose the pink, Swiss pearwood veneer underneath.

Stayman has set this textural pictorial scene within a carcass that reveals an exquisite sense of composition and restrained use of color. She deftly integrates the Swiss pearwood top and structural elements, curly maple broad flat sur-faces and cove molding around the top, and holly for delicate linear accenting into a unified piece with subtle historical Egyptian references.

1.   Biographical information from Stayman's response to author's questionnaire, January 1989; and her resume.
2.   Interview with the author, December 1988.
3.   Suzanne Meyer Spina, "Portfolio: Wendy Stayman," *The Workshop* 3 (fall 1983), p. 11.
4.   Conversation with the author, April 1989. See H.W. Janson, *History of Art*, 2nd ed. (New York: Harry N. Abrams, 1977), p. 60.

RICK WRIGLEY

24 SIDEBOARD
Holyoke, Massachusetts, 1989
Honduran mahogany, maple, ebony, medium-density fiberboard; pomele sepele, rosewood, curly sycamore, maple veneers; black Andes granite, patinated copper, brass
H: 39¾ in., W: 42¼ in., D: 21¾ in.
Loaned by Rick Wrigley

During the height of classically inspired Post-Modernism in the early 1980s, Rick Wrigley (b. 1955) sought inspiration from historical examples to develop rich and meaningful work that provided relief from the chaotic environment of the late twentieth century. Rather than use the past in a superficial, aesthetic manner as many architects and designers did, Wrigley intensively studied the forms, proportions, and detailing of the best old work and combined these insights with a sophisticated knowledge of techniques and materials to "recontinue" the traditions of Duncan Phyfe, Charles Honore Lannuier, and Thomas Hope from the early nineteenth century and of Herter Brothers, Daniel Pabst, and other makers of artistic furniture from the late nineteenth century.[1] He has become a master of veneer, inlay, and marquetry using exotic woods and other media.

Wrigley grew up in a middle-class environment with little or no exposure to woodworking or the craft movement.[2] At age 20, however, he apprenticed with an English-trained cabinetmaker in Fairfax, Virginia, who operated a shop engaged mostly in architectural woodwork. Wrigley was attracted to furnituremaking because it provided a sense of continuity with the past and a challenge of logical, methodical problem solving. His own work featured natural-finish hardwoods in the mid-1970s style inspired by James Krenov and Wharton Esherick.[3] With a solid introduction to wood and cabinetmaking, Wrigley decided to attend the School for American Craftsmen at Rochester Institute of Technology (RIT).

Wrigley began his studies at RIT in 1977. The curriculum emphasized technique and provided him with a wide knowledge ranging from hand tools to jigs to machines, but Wrigley was less pleased with the instruction in design. In the late 1970s, the RIT design philosophy remained rooted in the Danish modern aesthetic of the 1950s and paid very little attention to furniture history, especially that before the Art Deco work of the 1920s and 1930s.

Fig. a. Sideboard. William Hook (1777–1867). Salem, Massachusetts, 1808–1809. Mahogany, white pine, birch; satinwood, rosewood, mahogany veneers. H: 42¾ in., W: 48 in., D: 23⅞ in. Museum of Fine Arts, Boston. Bequest of Mabel H.F. McInnes 38.67.

Wrigley graduated from RIT in 1981 and moved to New Rochelle, New York. There he set up his own business in a space shared with Ron Trumble. He concentrated on interior architectural work, both business and residential, to pay his rent while doing an occasional piece of furniture for a show. Workbench Gallery, in particular, showed this exhibition work, most of which explored irony or had humorous touches. One of his most publicized works of this genre was his ironic armoire for the 1984 "Material Evidence: New Color Techniques in Handmade Furniture" show. The neo-Palladian structure consisted of a doored storage area between two

Corinthian columns, surmounted by a frieze with arabesque decoration. ColorCore sides were painted in places to imitate stucco flaking away from the "stone walls," and the *trompe l'oeil* painted frieze imitated carving.[4] He soon tired of his show work, and began to believe that such ironic work was an easy acceptance of crude or awkward design and workmanship and that good historically inspired works were very challenging.

Essential to Wrigley's perspective was his increased involvement with architectural firms. Judy Coady, then director of the Workbench Gallery, had brought Wrigley's work to the attention of the interior designer Patricia Conway of Kohn Pedersen Fox Conway (KPFC). Conway was impressed and tapped Wrigley for a conference table for the New York headquarters of Home Box Office. Made in 1984, the HBO table was Wrigley's first of many architectural commissions.[5] The architectural firm based the design concept on the graphics of a Frank Lloyd Wright stained glass window, but Wrigley worked with the basic geometry and provided delicate touches in the inlaid craftsmanship and the exquisitely balanced materials: exotic mahoganies, green Verdi marble, mother-of-pearl, and sterling silver. The table represented Wrigley's first real effort at the two-dimensional decorative effect of inlay. Working with KPFC made Wrigley aware of his own shallow design vocabulary and spurred him to look more closely at the furniture of Frank Lloyd Wright, the German Jugendstil, the Austrian Secessionists, the Aesthetic Movement, and neoclassicism. From these sources Wrigley developed the geometrically patterned inlay and mixed media highlights of the HBO table.

Finding the cost of living and working in the New York area prohibitive, Wrigley moved to Holyoke. Like James Schriber in New Milford, Connecticut, Wrigley has found it easy to maintain New York architectural contacts while working in more affordable studio space. Within a year of his move to Holyoke, he received a commission from Russell Gibson von Dohlen Architects and the Connecticut Commission on the Arts to make forty-four doors for the hearing rooms in the Connecticut Legislature Office Building. For this project Wrigley developed his own design combining veneer, inlay, and marquetry and decorating the stiles and rails of each door with 240 black oxide rivets (fig. b). This latter element was inspired by Thomas Hope's admiration for the brass-studded doors in Florence. The sheer quantity of doors and the meticulous

Fig. b.   Door (1 of 22 pairs). Holyoke, Massachusetts, 1989. Cherry; quilted mahogany, walnut, maple, rosewood, pearwood, ebony, anigre, holly veneers; mother-of-pearl, black oxidized rivets. H: 108 in., W: 72 in., D: 2 in. Connecticut Legislative Office Building, Hartford, Connecticut.

work on each required Wrigley to expand his work force to five assistants. Subsequent commissions through KPFC and other architectural firms have kept Wrigley's shop active producing custom-design, finely executed, and richly detailed conference tables, reception desks, and executive desks. He still fits in an occasional speculative piece for a show, but such work remains consistent with the designerly tradition of his commissions (fig. c).

Wrigley's recent sideboard (cat. 24), his most ambitious speculative piece, brings together all of his achievements over the past five years.[6] After studying a sideboard by William Hook of Salem (fig. a), Wrigley became fascinated with the rich fanlike veneer of the facade and the elegant proportions that allowed a substantial carcass to appear light upon turned legs. Reducing the scale slightly, he retained the basic reeded leg shape (although he used a shaper jig to reed them), and introduced his own elements. He veneered a fan of curly sycamore and edged this with a marquetry border and banner holders derived from the intarsia floor of the Cathedral of Siena. On the top he used a rich black granite as a mixing surface and bordered it with cross-banded curly sycamore. He also veneered the drawer fronts with curly sycamore cut with wavy edges, resulting in a curly herringbone pattern. The sides and the area above the Sienese motif are veneered with pomele sepele, an exotically patterned mahogany. Finally Wrigley added patinated copper discs with brass caps to the legs and drawer pulls and patinated rivet heads to the lower rail to provide color and textural contrast to the wood surfaces. The use of veneer, inlay, and marquetry, together with metallic accents links the sideboard to his earlier commissions, but their use on a smaller scale demonstrates how successfully he has fit his late twentieth-century stamp upon traditional proportion and form. His personal work has thus become even more striking than his architectural commissions.

Fig. c.   Bedstead. Holyoke, Massachusetts, 1986. Maple; black oxidized screws. H: 50 in., W: 60 in., D: 80 in. Private collection.

3.   A table with tapered legs and a top reminiscent of Esherick's work is illustrated in *Fine Woodworking: Design Book Two* (Newtown: Taunton Press, 1979), p. 108.

4.   *Material Evidence: New Color Techniques in Handmade Furniture* (Washington, D.C.: Smithsonian Institution, 1985), p. 6.

5.   The table is illustrated and discussed in "Rick Wrigley: Dialogue with Architecture," pp. 60–61.

6.   Discussion of the sideboard is based on conversation with the author, June 1989.

1.   Wrigley uses the term "recontinue" very deliberately because he, like Richard Scott Newman, sees Modernism as a disruptive force that severed our sense of heritage: see Wrigley's response to author's questionnaire, June 1989. In the questionnaire, he also specified the cabinetmakers listed as the most important influences on his own work.

2.   Biographical information from questionnaire; "Rick Wrigley: Dialogue with Architecture," *American Craft* 48, no. 3 (June/July 1988), pp. 60–61 and 105; conversations with the author, December 1988 and June 1989; and his resume.

EDWARD ZUCCA

MYSTERY ROBOTS RIP OFF THE RAIN FOREST
Woodstock, Connecticut, 1989
Honduran mahogany, maple, yellow poplar; acrylic paint,
gesso, polyethylene ink
H: 31 in., W: 30½ in., L: 132 in.
Loaned by Edward Zucca

Edward Zucca (b. 1946) was one of the first studio furnituremakers to successfully reach beyond the inherent beauty of
wood to focus upon humor, satire, and irony. His ability to do
so without sacrificing design or structural integrity makes him
a pivotal figure in the transformation from woodworking to
furnituremaking.

Zucca's wide-ranging imagination and love of building
date back to his childhood and adolescence.[1] He fondly recalls
his collection of trinkets, space guns, and wind-up toys, and
remembers assembling hundreds of plastic models and building a myriad of structures with his Erector Set, Tinker Toys,
and Lincoln Logs. His interest in building and design led him
to pursue a career in architecture, but, after being rejected by
the University of Pennsylvania, he turned to art and enrolled at
the Philadelphia College of Art (PCA).

In the late 1960s PCA was a "crazy and exciting" environment in contrast to the suburban New Jersey of Zucca's childhood. PCA's foundation program included courses in two- and
three-dimensional design, anatomy, graphic design, painting,
drawing, drafting, printmaking, clay, metal, and wood. Zucca
found wood clean and easy to control, and the methodical,
step-by-step process of woodworking appealed to him. Working in wood did not involve heat, fire, or chemicals, and the
cumulative nature of the steps meant that a mistake or accident
did not usually ruin the whole project.

In his junior year, Zucca majored in wood with Dan
Jackson, minored in clay with Bill Daley, and continued to
study metal with Olaf Skoogfors. Jackson did not teach from a
historical perspective, but emphasized mastering basic cabinetmaking skills, thinking widely, and plugging into contemporary culture. When he graduated in 1968, Zucca's style
resembled one aspect of his mentor's work. He used traditional techniques to conceive the form, then added carving to
relate gracefully the individual parts and accentuate the tran-
sitions. This additive integration of technique and carving
linked Zucca to the Art Nouveau style rather than to the non-

Fig. a. Trestle table. Attributed to Benjamin Clark (1644-1724). Med-
field, Massachusetts, 1690-1720. Silver maple, white pine. H: 26³⁄₁₆ in.,
W: 24¾ in., L: 108½ in. Museum of Fine Arts, Boston. Helen and Alice
Coburn Fund and Frederick Brown Fund 1980.446.

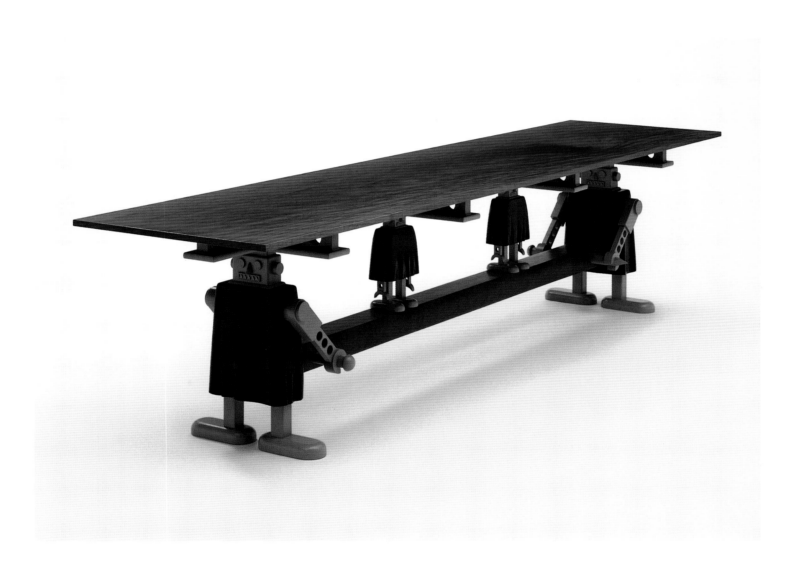

Fig. b. *Leaking Mirror*. Putnam, Connecticut, 1977. Walnut, basswood, plywood; mirror glass, silver leaf. H: 32 in., W: 44 in., D: 1½ in. Private collection.

Fig. c. *Shaker Television*. Putnam, Connecticut, 1979. Maple, basswood; zebra wood veneer; Shaker seat tape, gold leaf. H: 36 in., W: 24 in., D: 18 in. Private collection.

traditional techniques and subtractive shaping that characterized the work of Wendell Castle.

In 1971, a trip to Mexico changed Zucca's work dramatically. The geometric composition, massing, and ornament of Pre-Columbian architecture enthralled him and led him to develop his own personal style of making furniture. Pre-Columbian architecture and carving, along with Egyptian artifacts, Shaker furniture, Art Deco design, appliance and car design, and space fantasy toys of the 1940s and 1950s became part of his new vocabulary. *Leaking Mirror* of 1977 (fig. b) demonstrates his interest in narrative humor; *Shaker Television* of 1979 (fig. c) uses traditional Shaker details and joinery to set up an artifactual oxymoron; and *Electric Table #1* of 1979 (fig. d) is a good example of his attempts to merge a wood aesthetic with a fresh contemporary design.

Zucca expresses himself most easily in wood and relies on a repertoire of traditional woodworking skills: "If I can't make it out of wood, I'll change the design."[2] In a number of pieces, for example, Zucca has coated the wood with several layers of sanding sealer and sprayed a final surface of silver paint to produce the surface appearance of metal, an illusion given additional impact by the insertion of dowel buttons to simulate rivets. Other times he has painted wood to simulate patinated bronze or stone. Zucca's ornamental range is equally broad—he has used old Erector Set parts, Shaker seat tape, and even light-emitting diodes. He substituted the latter for inlays of exotic woods or semi-precious materials. A 1979 grant from the Connecticut Commission on the Arts provided him the opportunity to explore this role of electronics in furniture design. On one recent tall case clock, he veneered the entire surface with dollar bills and entitled it *Time is Money*.

Zucca's irreverent design is not accompanied by compromised technique. Admonished by Jackson not to "jeopardize structural integrity," Zucca's repertoire includes such traditional joints as dovetails and mortise and tenons; newer joints such as spline tenons and Lamello wafers; and various techniques for stabilizing large wood surfaces such as plywood cores, frame and panel construction, end battens, or floating screws.

Zucca relies on commissions to earn his living while making speculative work for gallery shows. He has had one-man shows at Snyderman and Workbench galleries, was included in the seminal "New Handmade Furniture" of 1979 and

"Craft Today: Poetry of the Physical" in 1986, and has participated in several shows each year.

In looking at the furniture collection at the Museum of Fine Arts, Zucca shied away from the most high-style objects. Instead he opted for the directness, simplicity, and proportions of a seventeenth-century trestle table (fig. a). In place of a "serious designed piece," he decided to build a "message piece." This choice was influenced by a giant eleven-foot board of Honduran mahogany that turned up at the lumber yard. He viewed it as a giant board from a great tree that should not have been cut down. At a time of growing concern over tropical deforestation and the greenhouse effect, Zucca linked the long table form and his giant board to make a piece of furniture that commented on the furnituremaker's guilt in using exotic or tropical wood (cat. 25).[3] To give the board the proper stage, he designed, built, and painted sinister robot figures who appeared to be marching away with the board. Carved and painted robots derived from wind-up toys carry a hewn tree, whose combed gessoed surface resembles bark. Zucca also included a favorite touch—a wooden understructure for the top that resembles space-age pierced metal girders. The entire table is constructed of wood, predominantly mahogany, with mortise-and-tenon joints. The plain treatment of the solid wood top contrasts well with the textured paint of the evil robots and their equipment. *Mystery Robots Rip Off the Rain Forest* thus demonstrates how Zucca successfully combines humorous elements to make social commentary in a non-threatening but thoughtful manner.

Fig. d. *Electric Table #1*. Putnam, Connecticut, 1979. Cherry, maple, ebony. H: 34 in., W: 21 in., D: 18 in. Private collection.

1. Biographical information from Zucca's response to author's questionnaire, December 1988; his resume; and Michael Stone, "Skill at Play: Edward Zucca," *American Craft* 41, no. 3 (June/July 1981), pp. 2–5.

2. Conversation with the author, June 1989.

3. On the deforestation concerns of furnituremakers, see George Putz, "Tropical Deforestation," and Lucinda Leech, "A Cabinetmaker Visits the Jungle," *Fine Woodworking* 70 (May/June 1988), pp. 80–85.